Doing RET

Joseph Yankura, Ph.D., received his doctoral degree in Clinical/School Psychology from Hofstra University and is a staff psychotherapist and approved training supervisor at the Institute for Rational-Emotive Therapy in New York City. He is a graduate of the Institute's fellowship training program; as a participant in this program he received clinical supervision from Dr. Albert Ellis and had the opportunity to co-lead therapy groups and workshops with him. Dr. Yankura is also a school psychologist in Long Beach, New York, and maintains a private practice in Merrick, New York.

Windy Dryden, Ph.D., is Senior Lecturer in Psychology at Goldsmiths' College, University of London. He has written and/or edited 35 books on rational-emotive therapy, cognitive-behavior therapy, and general psychotherapy. He is a Fellow of the Institute of Rational-Emotive Therapy and of the British Psychological Society, and is Consulting Editor of the *Journal of Cognitive Psychotherapy: An International Quarterly.*

Doing RET
Albert Ellis in Action

Joseph Yankura, Ph.D.
Windy Dryden, Ph.D.

SPRINGER PUBLISHING COMPANY
NEW YORK

Springer Publishing Company, Inc.
536 Broadway
New York, NY 10012

90 91 92 93 94 / 5 4 3 2 1

Library of Congress Cataloging-in-Publication Data

Yankura, Joseph
    Doing RET: Albert Ellis in Action /
Joseph Yankura, Windy Dryden.
        p. cm.
    Includes bibliographical references.
    ISBN 0-8261-6650-4
    1. Rational-emotive psychotherapy. 2. Ellis, Albert. I. Dryden,
Windy. II. Title.
    [DNLM: 1. Ellis, Albert. 2. Psychotherapy—methods. WM 420
Y23f]
RC489.R3Y36   1990
616.89′14—dc20
DNLM/DLC
for Library of Congress   90-9575
                                                             CIP

Printed in the United States of America

To Pat—

Thank you for your patience
and loving support

To Al—

Thank you for your wisdom
and guidance

Contents

ALBERT ELLIS

Foreword

This book, by Joseph Yankura and Windy Dryden, goes beyond anything that has yet been written about me and the manner in which I do psychotherapy. It especially emphasizes verbatim excerpts from some of my therapy sessions and thereby gives a unique first-hand picture of what I say and do as a therapist.

Other instances of my therapeutic style are given in Michael Bernard's *Staying Rational in an Irrational World: Albert Ellis and Rational-Emotive Therapy*, in Daniel Wiener's *Albert Ellis: Passionate Skeptic*, and in several of my own books, especially *Growth Through Reason, Humanistic Psychotherapy: The Rational-Emotive Approach*, and (with Windy Dryden), *The Practice of Rational-Emotive Therapy*. But the present book goes beyond this material and includes other aspects of my style and manner, as reported by the authors, by some of my clients, and by other observers. It is therefore the most complete picture of my therapy that has ever been published. Even I learned from it!

The only thing I would quibble about in the book is the impression it gives that I am somewhat lax about giving RET homework to my clients. This is partly true, because I often fail to tell these clients, "Let's give you this specific homework," or, "Let's, both of us, figure out what would probably be some effective RET homework for you." In fact, with some of them I almost never mention the word "homework," even when I assign it and they agree to carry it out. So when asked, "Does Dr. Ellis regularly assign and check on your homework?" they may give somewhat negative or vague answers. Let me, however, make a few points in this connection:

1. I tell virtually all my clients, during the first session, "We are giving you a number of pamphlets on RET; and, if you don't already have them, down at the desk get my books, *A New Guide to Rational Living* and *How to Stubbornly Refuse to Make Yourself Miserable About Anything—Yes, Anything!* As soon as you can, start reading the pamphlets and the books."

2. I also frequently recommend, as homework, some of my bestselling audiocassettes that the Institute for Rational-Emotive Therapy publishes—

especially, *Conquering the Dire Need for Love, Conquering Low Frustration Tolerance*, and *I'd Like to Stop But . . . Overcoming Addictions.*

3. I say to virtually all my clients, "The main thing you'll find valuable to do during the week is to make a brief note to yourself, writing down any unfortunate event that happens to you and the disturbed feeling—such as anxiety or depression—and the self-defeating behavior—such as procrastination and withdrawal—that you experience about this activating event. Just a short note to yourself, else you'll forget many of the bad things that occur and your feelings about them. Then we'll have plenty to discuss during your next session!"

4. I not only urge my clients, in between sessions, to dispute their irrational beliefs, but to do so strongly and repeatedly, and often to use our RET Self-Help Report Forms which they can pick up at the Institute's reception desk.

5. I sometimes neglect to check up on clients' specific agreed-upon homework—even though I usually make a note of it in their record—because I get too absorbed in some of the things they are telling themselves and in disputing their irrational beliefs. My forgetfulness in this respect is my problem—perhaps stemming from my own low frustration tolerance! For even I certainly do inelegant RET at times, showing that I am still a fallible human!

Otherwise, I think that this book is forceful, direct, and exceptionally clear. It tells almost "Everything You Ever Wanted to Know About Albert Ellis, But Were Afraid to Ask." I congratulate Joe Yankura and Windy Dryden on their honest, down-to-earth job!

Albert Ellis, Ph.D., President
Institute for Rational-Emotive Therapy

Preface

Dr. Albert Ellis is the founder of rational-emotive therapy (RET), perhaps the most widely practiced form of the cognitive-behavioral therapies. Among the various forms of psychotherapy in use today, RET can be considered unique for its ability to provide psychotherapy clients with an array of tools for alleviating emotional and behavioral problems within a relatively brief span of treatment time. Among contemporary psychotherapists, Ellis is unique in his emphases upon force, efficiency, humor, and deep-seated philosophical change within his therapeutic work. He is renowned not only as a psychotherapist, but also as an author, lecturer, and supervisor of psychotherapy trainees. His tireless efforts have had a profound impact upon the practice of clinical psychology; this fact was formally recognized by the American Psychological Association when it presented him with its award for Distinguished Professional Contributions to Knowledge in 1985.

At present, a fairly great number of books have been published on rational-emotive therapy. These publications are largely represented by self-help books and practitioners' manuals describing the application of RET to specific psychological problem areas and particular client populations. The practitioners' manuals often make reference to Ellis's work and style; such references, however, are widely scattered and have never before been collected and systematized. In fact, not a single published work existed which provided an organized and elaborated description of the manner in which Ellis practices RET.

The authors of the present volume considered this situation worthy of remediation. Through study of Ellis's actual in-session behaviors, students of psychotherapy might refine their own therapeutic skills and increase their understanding of the rational-emotive approach. In this vein, this book employs excerpts from transcripts of Ellis's psychotherapy sessions as the primary vehicle for illustrating his use of particular strategies and techniques with clients. In order to obtain useful transcript material, over one hundred audiotapes of Ellis's psychotherapy sessions were reviewed. This transcript material is supplemented and explained with frequent references to Ellis's voluminous writings on the practice of RET.

The book is organized in two sections: Part One is focused specifically upon describing the manner in which Ellis does RET, while Part Two mainly examines his approach to handling a number of issues generic to psychotherapy. The final chapters of both sections are based upon personal interviews with Ellis. In addition, Part Two includes a special chapter in which clients provide their reactions to his therapy. Overall, we believe that the format of this book will allow the reader to hear Ellis's therapeutic voice with unusual clarity.

The authors would like to express their gratitude to Dr. Ellis and the Institute for Rational-Emotive Therapy in New York City for the support and assistance provided for this project. We would also like to extend a special thank-you to the clients who volunteered to share their therapy experiences with us. By stepping forward to speak about what can be an intensely personal experience, they have each made a contribution to the literature on RET.

JOSEPH YANKURA, Ph.D.
WINDY DRYDEN, Ph.D.

PART I
DOING RET

1

The Origins, Theory, and Techniques of Rational-Emotive Therapy

Largely on the basis of my clinical experimentation, I forged ahead in the early 1950's to discover the gross ineffectuality of psychoanalysis and to develop more rational and distinctly more efficient techniques with my clients. And as I did so, I began to develop RET theory. (Ellis, 1977a, p. 4)

Albert Ellis is widely regarded as a master psychotherapist, as well as the premiere practitioner of rational-emotive therapy (RET). In order to best understand and appreciate his approach to doing psychotherapy, however, it is necessary to first have some basic knowledge of the principles and practice propositions of RET. Once such a foundation has been acquired, it becomes a relatively easy task to see how Ellis's actual in-session behaviors are quite appropriate to the therapeutic context within which they are set. Attempting to interpret these behaviors within the conceptual contexts provided by other, divergent forms of psychotherapy could lead to misunderstandings and uninformed rejections of Ellis's approach.

With the importance of conceptual contexts in mind, the present chapter will provide an outline of the theory and main techniques of RET. The reader acquainted with this body of factual knowledge will be well-equipped to explore the psychotherapy of Albert Ellis.

THE ORIGINS OF RATIONAL-EMOTIVE THERAPY

At the beginning of his career as a psychotherapist in the late 1940s and early 1950s, Ellis practiced classical psychoanalysis. He found, however, that the relatively passive techniques of this approach required a good deal of time to yield results, and that most of his clients were unable to afford as many sessions as they appeared to need. As such, he started to experiment with increasingly active and directive approaches, which in his estimation resulted in better therapeutic outcomes for his clients (Ellis, 1957). As he proceeded with this experimentation, he began to formulate the principles and techniques of rational-emotive therapy.

It is important to note that Ellis's formulation of RET was not based solely upon his early dissatisfaction with the psychoanalytic approach. Indeed, rational-emotive theory has both ancient and contemporary roots. Ellis acknowledges that his thinking has been influenced by the surviving writings of some of the ancient Stoic philosophers (such as Epictetus and Marcus Aurelius), as well as by the work of such modern psychologists as Alfred Adler and Karen Horney. As such, RET represents a unique synthesis of philosophy and psychotherapy. It is, in short, an unabashedly philosophically-based approach to psychotherapy. RET clients are helped to identify the dysfunctional aspects of their personal philosophies, and are taught the means by which they can adapt a philosophy of life that will lead to more optimal functioning.

At present, the primary site for the dissemination of Ellis's ideas is the Institute for Rational-Emotive Therapy, located in New York City.[1] Founded as a non-profit agency in 1959, the Institute offers training programs in RET for mental health professionals, public workshops dealing with a variety of issues germane to emotional and behavioral adjustment, and psychotherapeutic services within both individual and group contexts. Currently, the Institute also has branches in a number of major U.S. and foreign cities.

To date, hundreds of self-help books have appeared on the market which employ (albeit in an often unacknowledged way) rational-emotive principles. In addition, a large number of publications have appeared for practitioners which detail the application of RET to a wide variety of problem areas. These areas include alcoholism and substance abuse (Ellis, McInerney, DiGiuseppe, & Yeager, 1988), problems of childhood and adolescence (Bernard & Joyce, 1984), couples therapy (Ellis, Sichel, Yeager, DiMattia, & DiGiuseppe, 1989), family therapy (Huber & Baruth, 1989), and client resistance (Ellis, 1985a). It is also important to note that there now exists a body of literature which purportedly provides empirical support for the theoretical tenets of RET (Ellis, 1977b), as well as for its efficacy as a therapeutic approach (DiGiuseppe & Miller, 1977; McGovern & Silverman, 1984).[2]

THE BASIC THEORETICAL CONCEPTS OF RET

As noted above, RET is a philosophically-based approach to psychotherapy. As such, it views an individual's personal philosophy of life as being the main factor in determining whether that individual leads an existence filled with a maximum of pleasure and self-actualization, or one fraught with needless emotional misery and self-defeating behavior. From the RET perspective, it is not the negative events and adverse circumstances of our lives which cause maladjustment; rather, it is mainly our *beliefs* about such things which give rise to emotional and behavioral problems.

Rational-emotive theory holds that as human beings, we have inborn, biologically-based tendencies to maintain both *rational* and *irrational* beliefs about ourselves, others, and the world. Rational beliefs will usually lead to appropriate emotional and behavioral responses in the face of adversity, while irrational beliefs will most often result in inappropriate (and dysfunctional) responses. As we can exert some degree of control over the beliefs to which we subscribe, we also have the capacity to influence our own emotional and behavioral responses. Thus, RET does not view human behavior as being unduly influenced by the environment. In this vein, it can be regarded as offering a distinctly humanistic and largely non-deterministic theory of personality.

Rational-emotive theory offers rather precise definitions of rational and irrational beliefs, which makes it relatively easy for psychotherapy clients to learn how to distinguish between the two. Basically, rational thinking is considered to consist of beliefs that promote individual survival and happiness, while irrational thinking is said to consist of beliefs that create obstacles to these desirable outcomes (Ellis and Harper, 1975).

Based on the work of Ellis (1962, 1973a, 1979b; Ellis & Harper, 1975) and other rational-emotive theorists (Maultsby, 1975; Walen, DiGiuseppe, & Wessler, 1980; Wessler & Wessler, 1980) rational and irrational beliefs can be contrasted on a number of different dimensions, including the following:

Verifiability

Rational beliefs are largely based upon observable data, while irrational beliefs are not. Thus, it is possible to cite sound evidence to support the validity of rational beliefs. Irrational beliefs, on the other hand, cannot be supported by the facts. They are not based in reality. As an example, consider the following statement: "It is good to have the approval of other people; therefore, I *must* have this approval." The initial part of this thought would be considered rational, as we can find ample evidence to support the notion that it is beneficial to have the approval of others. The second part is clearly irrational, since there is no evidence to support the contention that one *must* have that which is desirable.

Demandingness

Irrational beliefs have a demanding, rigid, absolutistic quality to them, while rational beliefs have a more probabilistic flavor and most often merely reflect our preferences, desires, and wishes. Irrational thinking is frequently reflected in sentences which contain words and phrases such as *should, must, ought to*, and *need*, when these idioms are employed in a fashion which reflects a philosophy of absolutism and dogmatism. Such a philosophy refuses to accept the reality of circumstances as they actually exist. To illustrate, the phrase, "I wish it would stop raining" would be considered rational, since it merely states what an individual's preference might be. "It *must* stop raining" is irrational, because it is absolutistic and in conflict with reality.

Evaluative Conclusions

An individual's shoulds and musts will often serve as fallacious premises which lead him or her into making erroneous evaluative conclusions about people, events, and circumstances. According to Dryden and Ellis (1987), these erroneous evaluations fall into three major categories: global person-rating, awfulizing, and "I-can't-stand-it-itis." The form that the erroneous evaluations will take is determined by the irrational premises which precede them.[3] This relationship is illustrated in the following sequence:

Irrational Belief or Premise: "My husband *must* treat me with more consideration!"

Actual Event: Husband is a half-hour late in meeting wife for a dinner date.

Erroneous Evaluative Conclusion: "My husband acted inconsiderately again. Because he did that which he *must* not do, he's a totally worthless bum!" (Global person-rating)

Unlike irrational beliefs, rational beliefs will usually not lead to such exagerrated evaluations.

Emotional Consequences

Both rational and irrational beliefs can lead to negative emotions; however, irrational beliefs result in the types of negative emotions that will most often have a debilitating effect upon an individual's functioning. The negative emotions produced by rational beliefs, on the other hand, are less extreme and can actually facilitate effective functioning insofar as they provide the individual with an impetus for attempting to change modifiable aspects of a given situation. Within RET, debilitating negative emotions are referred to as *inappropriate* feelings, while facilitative negative emotions are labelled *appropriate* feelings (Ellis, 1973b, 1977a, 1980a). Emotional states such as anger, anxiety, depression, guilt, and shame fall into the inappropriate category; feelings such as concern, regret, disappointment, and sadness are considered to be appropriate emotions.

Behavioral Consequences

As stated above, irrational beliefs can lead to debilitating emotional states. These states are debilitating not only because they are strongly dysphoric, but also because they often contribute to a variety of associated behavioral problems. Thus, the individual plagued by guilt might engage in a number of self-punishing, self-destructive behaviors, the anxious person might behave in an avoidant fashion, and the individual who frequently becomes angry may act in an accusing and aggressive manner. Rational beliefs result in feelings that, although possibly still negative, enhance the probability of engaging in constructive problem-solving behaviors.

Goal Attainment

Most people want to have good interpersonal relationships, to fill their lives with a maximum of pleasure, and to make optimal use of their skills and talents. Because irrational beliefs produce inappropriate negative emotions and contribute to self-defeating behaviors they will often create significant obstacles to the attainment of these goals. Rational beliefs increase the probability of attaining such goals, as they usually result in self-enhancing feelings and behaviors.

Based upon his earlier experiences in practicing rational-emotive therapy, Ellis compiled a list of the most common irrational beliefs to which his clients typically appeared to subscribe. This list is reproduced throughout much of the RET literature, and usually contains between eleven and thirteen items. More recently, Ellis has offered a more concise means for conceptualizing irrational beliefs. According to this newer scheme, these beliefs can be categorized largely on the basis of whether they embody absolutistic demands directed at oneself, other people, or conditions as they exist in the world.

As noted earlier, RET regards the human capacity to think in both rational and irrational terms as being a biologically-based phenomenon

(Ellis, 1976, 1979a). Therefore, the potential to make ourselves emotionally disturbed is also viewed as being inborn. This position is based upon the following observations:

1. Emotional disturbance and/or self-defeating behavior appear to be pandemic across human societies. Throughout history and across the world, emotional disturbance can be seen to be a universal occurrence.
2. There is, apparently, no direct correspondence between environmental conditions and emotional adjustment. As such, individuals reared under optimal conditions may still turn out to be seriously emotionally-disturbed, while individuals raised within the most horrendous environments may grow into reasonably well-functioning adults. Behavioral genetic research on psychopathology provides some support for this position.
3. Emotionally-disturbed individuals often have an exceptionally difficult time in overcoming their self-defeating patterns of feelings and behavior. If emotional disturbance were merely a product of learning or conditioning, it seems likely that this difficulty would be considerably less extreme. The research literature on recidivism rates for psychotherapy clients can be considered as providing evidence in support of this observation.

While RET stresses that our tendency to create irrational beliefs is innate, it acknowledges that we *are* subject to the influences of environmental conditions and sociocultural variables. These factors, however, simply play a hand in determining the *form* that our particular set of irrational beliefs will take. In and of themselves, they do not *cause* irrational beliefs.

If one accepts the premise that irrational thinking and emotional disturbance stem mainly from our biologically-based tendencies, it naturally follows that remediation of these problems will require intense and consistent effort. This conclusion has important consequences for the process of psychotherapy, as it means that both client and therapist will have to utilize considerable force and energy (to employ Ellis's terminology) to achieve the desired end. Within RET, an initial component of this work involves assisting clients to gain an understanding as to the relationship between their thoughts, feelings, and behaviors. The section that follows provides details on a model that is used to attain this goal.

THE ABC MODEL OF EMOTIONS

RET is perhaps most well-known for its ABC model, which provides an easily understandable means for explaining the origins of emotional disturbance. In the most simplified form of this model, A stands for "Activating

Events" and refers to the individual's perceptions regarding past, present, or future events. B stands for "Beliefs," and subsumes both the individual's rational and irrational thinking about A. C stands for "Consequent Emotions and Behaviors," and refers to the emotional and behavioral consequences of holding particular beliefs at B.

The interrelationships between the various components of this model can best be illustrated with a hypothetical case example. Imagine that two individuals are required to give lectures before large audiences, and that they are both aware of the possibility that they might do poorly at this task. In anticipation of this potential outcome, these individuals could experience quite different emotional responses. Person #1, for instance, might feel pleasantly excited about being provided with an opportunity to refine her skills as a lecturer, and only mildly concerned about the chance that she will do badly. On the other hand, Person #2 could conceivably feel quite anxious about the possibility that he will give a poor performance.

What determines whether these individuals will feel excited and mildly concerned or uncomfortably anxious? Simply enough, it is the manner in which they *think* about their upcoming lectures. If Person #1 believes that it would be nice to give a well-received lecture but that it is not an absolute necessity to do so, then she will be much less likely to approach this endeavor in an anxious manner. If Person #2, however, not only believes that it is preferable to do well, but also that he therefore *must* do a good job and that he *has to* win the approval of his listeners in order to prove himself a worthwhile person, then he will most likely regard the possibility of failure as representing a genuine horror. With these cognitions in operation, he will approach the task before him with considerable dread and worry.

For both individuals in this case example, the A (Activating Event) is represented by the recognition that it is possible to give an unsatisfactory lecture, and so to gain the disapproval of one's audience. The C's (Consequent Emotions) in this illustration include excitement, mild concern, and anxiety. The B's fall into two categories (rational and irrational beliefs), and determine which C's will be experienced. Thus, Person #1 experiences positive and facilitative feelings because she believes that it is only preferable to do a good job (a rational belief), while Person #2 experiences dysfunctional and disruptive feelings because he believes that he *must* do well (an irrational belief).

Several important features of the ABC model can be highlighted with the foregoing illustration. First, it is apparent that A does not have to be an event that has already actually occurred—it can also be an anticipated event. Second, it is important to recognize that although both hypothetical individuals started out with the same perception ("I might give a poor lecture and be ill-received by my audience"), they wound up with distinctly different C's because of their respective beliefs about A. Finally, it can be seen that it is possible to simultaneously have both rational and irrational beliefs about any particular A. In this vein, Person #2 believed (1) "It is preferable to give a good lecture and attain the approval of my audience," and (2) "Because these things are preferable, I *must* achieve them."

According to the ABC model, an individual's initial C can also become an A for additional emotional upsets. Within rational-emotive theory, these additional upsets are referred to as *secondary symptoms*. Thus, Person #2 might recognize that he is anxious about the prospect of failure, and then create even further distress for himself by thinking about his anxiety in the following manner: "Oh my God, I can see that I'm terribly anxious about delivering this lecture! I *must* not be anxious because that will interfere with my doing a good job, and I *must* do a good job!" Telling himself that he *must* do a good job creates his first-order symptom of anxiety; convincing himself that he *must* not be anxious results in a secondary symptom, additional anxiety. In the same manner, it is possible for individuals to become depressed about their anxiety, anxious about their depression, depressed about their depression, and so on. These "problems about problems" can frequently block clients from dealing successfully with their primary symptoms; as such, rational-emotive therapists often find it desirable to first help their clients to overcome their secondary symptoms.

In order to determine the nature of a given client's operative irrational beliefs, the rational-emotive therapist attempts to be a most careful listener and observer. By being sensitive to sometimes subtle cues, the therapist begins to form (and to test) hypotheses regarding the particular irrational beliefs to which the client might subscribe. The task of diagnosis is, however, only a small part of the role played by the rational-emotive therapist. As will be described in the next section, the task of *teaching* is a major component of this role.

THE THERAPIST AS TEACHER

Rational-emotive therapists are interested in providing their clients with a comprehensive emotional education. Consequently, they function as concerned, active, and often quite directive teachers. They are equipped with a clear and coherent model for understanding and remediating emotional disturbance, and they try to convey this model in the most effective and efficient manner possible. Ultimately, their end goal is usually to assist clients in becoming "their own therapists" (Kanfer & Phillips, 1969). When clients have reached this point, it ideally means that they are able to carry on the work of therapy without the guidance and supervision of the therapist. They have learned the principal tenets and techniques of RET, and are generally able to employ them independently.

In order to help clients to attain this level of independent functioning, the rational-emotive therapist tries to get across several basic points which will contribute to an individual's emotional well-being. These points, which have elsewhere been referred to as the three main insights of RET (Ellis, 1962; Grieger & Boyd, 1980), can be detailed as follows:

Insight Number 1

Emotional disturbance and dysfunctional behavior are not due mainly to either past or current events. Rather, these phenomena stem primarily from the irrational beliefs which individuals employ when they think about these events.

Insight Number 2

Regardless of how we originally became disturbed, we remain disturbed in the present because we are continually reindoctrinating ourselves with the irrational beliefs we created (or acquired) in the past.

Insight Number 3

Even if we attain the two insights above (in terms of acknowledging our role in creating and maintaining our own disturbance), we will become significantly less disturbed only if we consistently and continually work at giving up our irrational beliefs.

Together, these three insights place the responsibility for emotional upsets squarely upon the shoulders of the client. While at first glance this message might seem to represent a rather harsh "put down" of the client, it can be noted that RET strongly encourages clients not to berate themselves for holding irrational beliefs and for being emotionally disturbed. Disturbance, after all, is largely the result of our inborn human tendencies. Tremendously liberating consequences can accrue for the client who understands and accepts the above insights, as they can lead to the following conclusion: With effort, almost every person can overcome present-day emotional and behavioral problems, and can prevent future ones from occurring.

In addition to these three insights, the rational-emotive therapist also attempts to teach the following:

1. Emotions can be classified according to whether they are functional or dysfunctional. In this vein, recall the earlier distinction that was made between appropriate and inappropriate emotions (see pp. 6–7).

2. It is almost always possible to understand the origin of inappropriate emotions. With regard to this point, the therapist may choose to explicitly teach the client the ABC model. On the other hand, especially with brighter clients, the features of this model may merely be implied as the therapist repeatedly encourages the client to examine his or her thinking during the course of therapy.

3. Once upset-producing beliefs have been identified, it is possible to employ a variety of techniques for replacing them with more rational, functional beliefs. The nature of these techniques will receive treatment in the section to follow.

4. Positive changes in feelings or behavior that the client experiences during the course of therapy can often be traced back to modifications in his or her belief system. Such modifications are not in any way due to the "magical" curative powers of the therapist, and can certainly be accomplished (using the techniques referred to in #3) by the client on an independent basis.

5. As the tendency to create irrational beliefs is inborn, it is unlikely that it can ever be completely eradicated in any given individual. As such, it is to be expected that additional upsets will be experienced in the future, even if therapy has been "successful." Using RET techniques, clients may be able to overcome these future upsets on their own. They had best not, however, be unreasonably demanding of themselves regarding their use of these techniques.

THERAPEUTIC TECHNIQUES EMPLOYED IN RET

The major thrust of RET is to help clients to attain a lifestyle and level of functioning that is relatively free from serious emotional upsets and self-defeating behaviors. In order to accomplish this goal, they are taught the relationship between thoughts and feelings, and they learn how to identify and replace their self-sabotaging irrational beliefs. The process of *disputation* represents the means by which modifications in the client's belief system can be effected. Thus, the ABC model can be expanded to include D (for Disputing) and E (which stands for more adaptive emotional and behavioral Effects).

Basically, disputation refers to a number of techniques by which the client finds evidence to refute the irrational beliefs which he or she maintains. If consistently confronted with strong evidence for the falsity of a given belief, it is likely that an individual will reject this belief in favor of one that appears to be more representative of reality. By repeatedly disputing their upset-producing irrational beliefs, clients can help themselves to approach a more rational philosophy. Theoretically, this can result in significant improvements in affect. Disputation techniques fall into three major categories: cognitive, behavioral, and emotive.

Cognitive Disputation

Cognitive techniques for disputing are often employed by rational-emotive therapists from the very first session of therapy. The therapist will attempt to identify the client's irrational beliefs, and will then present arguments to demonstrate that these beliefs are not true. These arguments can be presented in a Socratic manner, whereby the therapist asks a series of thought-provoking questions which enable clients to generate valid conclusions on their own, or they may be presented didactically, in the form of mini-lectures. Generally, it is most desirable to attain some balance between these two methods, as this will help the therapist to direct the session while at the same time allowing the client to be an active participant within it.

By observing the therapist's example and by listening to his or her explanations regarding the means by which disputation is accomplished, clients learn how to use cognitive disputation outside of the therapy sessions. In so doing, they accumulate a repertoire of disputing questions that they can apply to their identified irrational beliefs:

Where is the evidence for this belief?
Is that really true?
Why *must* it be so?
Is there another way to think about this?
What's the worst thing that could happen? Would that *really* be awful?
What's this way of thinking about things going to get me?

The process of disputation can sometimes be greatly facilitated by employing a written format, especially when several irrational beliefs are involved in an episode of emotional distress. In this vein, the Institute for Rational-Emotive Therapy publishes a self-help form which clients can use for analyzing their upsets according to the ABC model (Sichel & Ellis, 1984).

RET makes a distinction between *elegant* and *inelegant* disputation. With the former, disputation is aimed specifically at the shoulds, musts, and have tos that are at the core of disturbance. Inelegant disputation, however, deals only with the faulty inferences (or distorted perceptions) that may result from one's irrational beliefs. Elegant disputation is, of course, considered preferable, as it eliminates a major source of such inferences.

In addition to cognitive disputation, clients receiving RET may also be taught how to use *rational self-statements* as another means for dealing with irrational beliefs. A rational self-statement is simply a sentence or phrase that reflects a more logical and realistic view of a given issue. Rather than using a series of disputing questions to prove the invalidity of an irrational belief, clients can often effect changes in their feelings merely by countering an irrational message with a more rational one. This approach is generally regarded as being a less effective vehicle for implementing deep-seated philosophic change, as it doesn't require the client to show him or herself *why* a particular belief is irrational. It can, however, prove quite useful for very young or intellectually-limited clients who lack the resources to dispute.

Behavioral Disputation

Evidence for the invalidity of irrational beliefs does not have to be obtained solely through arguments that one conducts "in one's head." It is also possible to obtain such evidence by *acting against* the beliefs that produce dysfunctional behavior patterns. In other words, by engaging in behaviors that run counter to the tendencies resulting from their irrational beliefs, clients can provide themselves with more concrete "proof" that there are alternative ways of thinking about emotionally-charged issues.

With *risk-taking exercises*, clients are encouraged to engage in behaviors that they erroneously think will result in unbearable or dangerous consequences. Frequently, when they finally force themselves to undertake such an exercise, they learn that the feared outcome is not at all "awful" and that they are quite well able to handle it. As an example of this principle, take the hypothetical case of a young man who is extremely fearful of being rejected when he asks a woman out for a date. Given the existence of this fear, the RET therapist would suggest to this client that he believes he "must have the approval of those whom he considers significant," and would encourage him to act against this must by actually going out and "collecting" rejections. With repeated exposure to such experiences, this client could eventually teach himself that he can indeed survive rejection. Thus, he would learn that he doesn't *need* to be accepted.

Incidentally, risk-taking exercises can sometimes have positive side effects for clients. In the hypothetical case described above, for instance, it is unlikely that the client would be rejected by each and every woman whom he might ask out. As some will probably accept his invitations, he will (1) gain additional dating experience, and (2) discover that the more invitations he extends, the more dates he will have. As such, risk-taking exercises can sometimes present clients with no-lose situations.

Shame-attacking exercises are another vehicle for conducting behavioral disputing. Here, the client is instructed to purposely engage in silly and outlandish (but non-harmful to self and others) behaviors in public. By implementing such assignments, it is possible to learn that one doesn't have to take the disapproval of others *too* seriously, as this can rarely be harmful in any significant or enduring way. In addition, clients can help themselves to acquire the beneficial insight that no matter how poorly they might behave, they don't have to engage in self-denigration. RET therapists generally have a stock of shame-attacking exercises that they might suggest to clients, including the following:

1. Walking down the street with an open umbrella on a sunny day.
2. Calling out the stops on the subway in a loud voice.
3. Stopping a stranger on the street and saying, "Excuse me, I've just gotten out of the loony bin. Can you tell me what year it is?"

Emotive Disputation

Cognitive disputation focuses mainly upon an individual's thinking processes, while behavioral disputation has an action orientation. As defined here, emotive disputation involves teaching the client to utilize imagery experiences to produce various affective states. These states then become the starting point for the process of effecting therapeutic cognitive modifications. *Rational-Emotive Imagery* (Maultsby & Ellis, 1974) is the primary technique by which emotive disputing is conducted. There are two versions of this technique, one of which employs negative imagery, the other of which utilizes positive imagery.

In the negative imagery version (which is the one which Ellis employs most frequently), clients are asked to close their eyes and imagine, as vividly as they can, a situation which for them is usually associated with emotional upsets. After achieving this, they are then requested to allow themselves to experience the typical emotional upset with which they respond to this situation. Once they have signalled to the therapist that this has been accomplished, they are instructed to change their inappropriate negative emotion into an appropriate negative emotion. Then, they are asked to describe how they accomplished this change. Ideally, they will respond by reporting that they modified some aspect of the manner in which they were thinking about the situation.

With the positive imagery version, clients again use their imagination to place themselves in a difficult situation. After allowing themselves to experience the upsets usually associated with this situation, they then attempt to identify and dispute their operative irrational beliefs. Finally, they attempt to picture, through fantasy, how they would tend to feel and act after giving up these irrational beliefs. This last component of the exercise is likely to involve "positive" types of images (i.e., images of oneself feeling and acting in more appropriate ways), and is the reason that this variation on the technique is referred to as the positive imagery version.

Rational-emotive imagery can serve as an in-session demonstration to clients that they *can* exert control over their feelings, and that focusing on changing some aspect of their thinking represents the most effective and efficient way of doing so. It can be recommended to clients that they practice the technique between sessions, as this will assist them in refining their disputing skills. In addition to helping individuals to overcome upsets connected with past events, rational-emotive imagery is also intended to be useful as a means for inoculating oneself against upsets that are anticipated in future situations.

A distinctly emotive element can be added to cognitive disputing when it is practiced in an especially forceful and vigorous manner. The impact of a disputing question can be greatly augmented, for instance, when it is phrased in language and given an inflection that is highly evocative for the individual. Consider the relative impact of the following two sentences:

1. Why must I be certain I'll get the promotion?
2. Why the FUCK *must* I be certain I'll get the promotion?

OTHER TECHNIQUES UTILIZED WITHIN RET

Lazarus (1967, 1976) has stressed the desirability of technical eclecticism within psychotherapy. While RET emphasizes the importance of disputation in attaining positive therapeutic outcomes, it also attempts to provide a comprehensive approach to treatment by incorporating techniques derived from many other orientations to psychotherapy. Operant conditioning techniques and skills-training approaches, for example, are often included within a rational-emotive treatment package.

With regard to operant conditioning techniques, clients may be encouraged to establish contingencies for themselves which might help them to complete difficult tasks. Thus, the client who wishes to practice rational-emotive imagery on a daily basis may choose to reward herself by playing racketball after she has done so. Further, she may decide to withhold this activity from herself until she accomplishes that which she wishes to do. In addition, she may set herself a penalty (in the form of some activity which she despises, such as cleaning the bathroom) if she doesn't complete her assignment by a certain hour of the day.

Skills training approaches may be applied to a wide variety of client problems. The overly submissive client would probably benefit from some assertiveness training, while the shy client might be assisted by some instruction in conversational skills. General problem-solving skills such as those described by D'Zurilla (1986) are also quite useful at times, insofar as they teach clients how to become more flexible thinkers in generating alternative solutions to the dilemmas which they encounter.

HOMEWORK ASSIGNMENTS IN RET

Generally speaking, RET clients (as well as clients receiving many other types of psychotherapy) receive one hour of therapy per week. In order to make good use of the 167 hours remaining in the week, rational-emotive therapists suggest to clients that they undertake various types of homework assignments. Such assignments serve to make therapy more effective and efficient, as they function as a means for extending treatment time. In addition, they can serve to foster client independence, as they are intended to be implemented in the therapist's absence.

At the beginning of therapy, the therapist is often quite directive in terms of giving explicit suggestions and instructions regarding the types of assignments the client is to carry out. As therapy progresses, however, the client ideally becomes an active collaborator in formulating the homework tasks. This approach (i.e., gradually shifting the responsibility for designing homework assignments from the therapist to the client) can be explained to clients at the outset of treatment, so that they don't mistakenly perceive the therapist as acting in an authoritarian manner.

A rational-emotive homework assignment will frequently consist of an activity designed to assist clients in the process of disputing and replacing their irrational beliefs. Hence, this type of homework can be cognitive, behavioral, or emotive in nature. Homework assignments might also provide opportunities to practice new skills, such as time management or assertiveness. Ultimately, the nature of homework assignments is limited only by the therapist's creativity and desire to see the client progress in therapy.

The foregoing chapter has described the basic principles and techniques of rational-emotive therapy. Hopefully, it has also conveyed some fundamental knowledge regarding the procedures utilized by rational-emotive therapists within therapy sessions. It is important to note, however, that not all practitioners of RET implement these procedures in the same fashion. There is, in fact, considerable variability between rational-emotive therapists with regard to style and approach.

The subsequent chapters will attempt to provide a clear and complete portrayal of the manner in which Albert Ellis conducts RET, and to illustrate the manner in which he is unique among psychotherapists.

NOTES

1. According to the catalog published by the Institute, "The Institute for Rational Living, a non-profit educational organization, was founded in 1959; the Institute for Rational-Emotive Therapy, offering professional training and clinical services, was founded in 1968. Today, the two Institutes are merged into one comprehensive, multi-service facility."

2. A number of reviewers have expressed criticisms regarding the treatment outcome literature on RET. Haaga and Davison (1989), for example, have noted that research on Beck's (1976) cognitive therapy has been progressing in a more rapid and systematic manner than the research on RET. They also point out the difficulty of assessing key rational-emotive constructs (such as irrational beliefs), and the fact that a standard RET treatment protocol does not exist for research purposes. These problems, among others that they mention, increase the difficulty of drawing valid conclusions concerning RET's effectiveness from the available outcome research.

3. Theoretically, individuals are likely to arrive at these erroneous evaluative conclusions when conditions are not as they believe they *must* be. Global person-rating refers to the process of attaching an evaluation of worth to oneself or other individuals, usually based upon some aspect of the person's behavior. Awfulizing refers to the process of evaluating particular circumstances as "awful," when this connotes that these conditions are more than merely unfortunate or inconvenient. "I-can't-stand-it-itis" refers to the process of erroneously concluding that particular conditions are absolutely intolerable.

2

Setting the Stage:
The Initial Session

I am exceptionally verbally active with my patients, especially during the first few sessions of therapy. I do a great deal of talking rather than passively listening to what the patient has to say. I do not hesitate, even during the first session, directly to confront the patient with evidences of his or her irrational thinking and behaving. (Ellis, 1967, p. 212)

Regardless of therapeutic orientation, psychotherapists typically attempt to accomplish several important tasks during their first meeting with a new client. They will, for instance, attempt to engage the client in the process of therapy, thus increasing the probability that a subsequent session will be scheduled. They will endeavor to convey confidence and inspire hope, and will work at establishing an alliance wherein it is understood that client and therapist are working together toward meaningful goals. They will try to obtain a sense of the nature and extent of the client's problems, and will begin formulating hypotheses regarding the strategies and techniques most likely to be beneficial. Finally, they will usually make some attempt at actually starting the work of helping the client to find relief from his or her presenting symptoms. While some degree of overlap exists between these various therapeutic tasks, it is safe to say that their completion requires a considerable amount of effort on the part of the therapist. Accomplishing these tasks is made all the more difficult by the fact that therapists usually work under severe time constraints: Most individual therapy sessions last no longer than one hour.

Despite the fact that Ellis typically meets with clients for sessions that are only one-half hour long, review of his audiotaped sessions suggests that he often manages to accomplish the above tasks in a most thoroughgoing manner. The present chapter will attempt to describe the means by which he does so. In the section that follows, issues pertaining to the relationship Ellis establishes with clients will receive consideration.

ESTABLISHING THE THERAPEUTIC RELATIONSHIP

Numerous theoretical systems have been proposed in the attempt to explain and define the relationship which exists between a psychotherapist and a client. The social power typology devised by Strong and Matross (1973) is one such system. It makes reference to therapist "power bases," and identifies the expert, referent, and legitimate bases as the main sources of the therapist's power to influence the client during the course of therapy. Expert power refers to the client's perception that the therapist possesses superior knowledge and information, which will be of use in overcoming his or her presenting complaints. Referent power, on the other hand, refers to the client's liking for and attraction to the therapist. Legitimate power originates with the client's belief that the therapist (by virtue of his or her societal role) has a "right" to influence the client's behavior.

It seems clear that Ellis operates largely from the expert base in his relationships with clients. More specifically, he employs his considerable knowledge and reputation as an expert in the service of establishing a working therapeutic alliance. As such, he generally does not rely upon the strategies psychotherapists may typically use to get clients to "like" them.

Many individuals who come to Ellis for therapy already have some sense of his stature within the field of psychotherapy; it is likely that these clients respond to him as an expert almost from the moment that they enter his office.[1] To clients who are unfamiliar with his reputation, Ellis establishes his expertise in a number of different ways. First, he is quite business-like and allows almost no time for small talk during his therapy sessions. Thus, it is likely that most of his clients quickly get a sense that he is there to help them, rather than to socialize with them. Second, but perhaps most importantly, he is very active during his sessions. As soon as the client has responded to his curt directive to "Be seated; make yourself comfortable," Ellis generally begins the work of determining the nature of the problems for which this individual is seeking help at the present time. He identifies distressing emotional states and dysfunctional behaviors, advances specific hypotheses as to the irrational beliefs that are causing and maintaining these difficulties, and attempts to engage the client in the types of philosophical arguments intended to facilitate cognitive change and bring about some degree of symptom-relief.

In addition to the types of verbal activity referred to above, Ellis also makes frequent reference to some of the trappings which can accompany expertise in a given professional field. Thus, he will often be heard making reference to his self-help writings during the course of a therapy session. Most of his initial sessions end, in fact, with the client being directed to obtain and read some of these materials. This assignment probably serves to augment his expert status in the client's eyes because of both its form (a direct suggestion) and content (a reference to his professional work).

Ellis's business-like approach and verbal style are likely to violate the expectancies of a good number of first-time clients who are not familiar with his manner. Unfortunately, it is the case that the general public's impressions of appropriate therapist behavior are based largely upon mass media portrayals. As such, "naive" clients may enter Ellis's office expecting this master therapist to be an unusually warm human being who will passively listen (while making an occasional sage comment) as they actively give vent to their concerns, complaints, and fears. Needless to say, they are in for a disappointment: Ellis is anything but passive in his work; in addition, he employs therapist "warmth" in a most discretionary manner.

It is widely recognized that therapist warmth can be a valuable tool for engaging clients in the therapeutic relationship. When the therapist displays overt signs of friendliness and "liking" toward the client, the latter will often respond in a similar fashion to the therapist. Thus, the probability of a subsequent session being scheduled is likely to be increased. This results in obvious economic advantages for therapists in private practice, and creates an opportunity to provide helpful intervention to individuals who might be in considerable distress. Despite these advantages, Ellis tends to downplay displays of warmth in his therapy sessions. In his view, a therapist who relies too heavily upon warmth in the therapeutic relationship is running the risk of impeding the therapy and doing a disservice to the client.

In a number of articles and interviews, Ellis has stated his observation that an overreliance upon displays of warmth and liking may serve to feed into clients' irrational beliefs that they *need* the love and acceptance of significant others (Dryden & Ellis, 1985; Ellis, 1967; Ellis, 1982; Weinrach & Ellis, 1980). If these beliefs are inadvertently strengthened by therapy, clients will be more likely to continue to upset themselves when they experience rejections. In addition, Ellis is concerned that therapist warmth can encourage clients to subscribe to a philosophy of conditional self-acceptance. Here, clients may believe that they are worthwhile individuals *because* their warmly-relating therapist seems to approve of them. This belief is distinctly at odds with rational-emotive philosophy, which holds that the unconditional acceptance of self and others is much more conducive to emotional adjustment. Finally, Ellis has noted that a therapeutic relationship characterized by an abundance of warmth and love may interfere with two important tasks of particular concern to rational-emotive therapists: Teaching and confrontation (Hoellen & Ellis, 1986). Overly warm therapists may tend to gloss over their clients' errors and inadequacies, rather than trying to help them recognize and remediate them.

It should be noted that Ellis is not totally opposed to displays of warmth by the therapist within therapy sessions. Rather, he regards the issue as representing a quandary for the therapist, particularly when working with a suicidal or otherwise very vulnerable individual. The nature of the predicament is perhaps best illustrated by this quote from an interview with Ellis:

> There are some people who are suicidal and others who are very vulnerable who, if you say anything harsh to them or if you try to push them to do uncomfortable things, just don't seem to be able to take it. So at the beginning of therapy with some people, I lean over backwards to be kinder than I might normally be. I still show them the ABC's of RET and encourage them to do active disputing. But I highlight some of their good traits and push them in the direction of hope. I still have a dilemma because I never know exactly where to draw the line. (Dryden & Ellis, 1985, p. 10)

As with most of the positions he has adopted regarding the practice of effective therapy, Ellis's opinions on the use of warmth are non-dogmatic and relativistic. From the passage excerpted above, one can draw the implication that it is best for the therapist to exercise vigilance and judgment with regard to employing behaviors that convey warmth.

Ellis's views regarding the appropriate degree of client/therapist collaboration within the therapeutic relationship also deserve consideration, as they have a significant impact on the nature of the alliance he establishes with his clients. He questions the notion of unqualified "therapeutic consumerism," wherein the therapist collaborates with the client on an equal basis to work toward fulfilling the client's agenda for therapy. He believes that such an approach can result in less efficient and effective treatment, as it requires the therapist to be less active and directive than he or she might otherwise be. Ellis does not hesitate to direct clients toward working on what he sees as being their most significant problems, and is quite active in showing them the underlying roots of their disturbance. From his perspective, it is unlikely that clients would present themselves for therapy in the first place if they did not require such overt guidance and teaching.

As noted earlier, Ellis's behaviors within therapy sessions are likely to be incongruent with the expectancies of a number of his first-time clients. For clients who are particularly rigid in their beliefs regarding the way a therapist "should" act, this incongruence may contribute to their concluding that Ellis will be unable to help them—as such, it is unlikely that a subsequent session will be scheduled. It is also probably true, however, that a good number of Ellis's clients leave his office after their first session believing that he understands their problems and is vitally concerned with helping them to effect meaningful changes in their lives.

If Ellis's displaysof warmth within sessions are relatively infrequent, how does he go about conveying concern for clients' problems? Review of the client interview material obtained for Chapter 12 ("How Clients View Their Therapy With Ellis") suggests that his active-directive style and level of alertness during sessions are largely responsible for clients' perceptions that he "cares" about helping them. As per the quote which opens the present chapter, Ellis tends to be "exceptionally verbally active" during his earlier therapy sessions with a given individual. As this verbal activity is highly-focused upon problem identification and remediation, it would be difficult for most clients to label his demeanor as apathetic during their initial session with him. Ellis manages to make it clear that his energies are directed at helping them to obtain relief from the distress which drove them to therapy.

APPROACHES TO ASSESSMENT
AND INTERVENTION DECISIONS

Ellis does not make use of the accepted taxonomy for psychiatric diagnoses outlined in the American Psychiatric Association's Diagnostic and Statistical Manual of Mental Disorders (DSM III-R 1987). In his view, the categories contained in this publication are too rigid and narrow to be of much practical use in terms of treatment planning for individual clients. In addition, he eschews extensive history-taking and the use of projective and objective personality tests as vehicles for gathering meaningful information about clients. To quote from his writings, he has stated that ". . . the best mode of diagnosis is therapy itself, since the ways in which the client reacts to the first few therapy sessions tells much more about him than any amount of objective or projective tests" (Saltzman & Ellis, 1986, p. 278).

By observing a given client's responses to his activities within the therapy session, Ellis draws inferences regarding the nature of the individual's major irrational beliefs, and is also able to make many of the clinical distinctions usually necessary to conduct effective therapy. He is, for example, able to distinguish the "difficult customers" (his label for individuals who resist or otherwise respond poorly to therapy) from the more compliant clients. This is critical information to possess, as it will influence clinical decisions regarding therapeutic strategies and style.

Despite his emphasis upon in-session observations and his view that extensive history-taking is usually unnecessary, Ellis *does* utilize the first session to obtain certain types of background information about clients. Thus, he will make inquiries as to the client's functioning with regard to social relationships, work performance, and love/sexual relationships. Although these inquiries are generally kept brief, they can provide Ellis with information that allows him to identify potential areas of focus for therapy. While the issues which are having the most immediate adverse impact upon the client are generally treated first, Ellis will often initiate discussions of other potential problem areas later in the course of therapy. He appears to have excellent recall for the details of particular cases, which he supplements with telegraphic session notes maintained on several rolodex files in his office. Clients may, of course, elect not to work on their additional problem areas once they have attained some relief from their most pressing emotional and behavioral difficulties; nevertheless, Ellis offers them the opportunity to extend their application of RET to numerous other spheres of functioning.

The content of the Biographical Information Form (Ellis, 1968; see Table 2.1) distributed to all new clients at the Institute for Rational-Emotive Therapy in New York City provides further insights as to the types of background information which Ellis considers germane to the therapeutic process. In addition to assessing such standard information as the client's age, marital status, and referral source, this form requires clients to:

1. Rate how religious they are on a scale ranging from "1" (for very religious) to "9" (for atheistic).
2. Report the number of years of formal education they have completed and the nature of their present occupation.
3. Indicate the types and amounts of prior treatment (including psychotropic medications and psychiatric hospitalizations) they have received for emotional problems.
4. List past and present complaints, symptoms, and problems.
5. Describe the respective conditions under which their problems are improved or exacerbated.
6. Describe relationships with significant family members.
7. Indicate the number of close relatives who have experienced significant emotional disturbance.

With regard to religiousness ratings, Ellis (1986a) has hypothesized that a relationship exists between religiosity (or rigid adherence to a prescribed set of values and/or religious beliefs) and susceptibility to emotional disturbance. Thus, these ratings can provide clues as to a variable which might present a source of resistance within RET. Years of formal education and present occupation can lead to inferences regarding the client's level of intellectual functioning (which can receive validation through observations of intra-session behavior), while information regarding prior treatment, past and present symptomatology, and familial emotional disturbance can lend itself to hypotheses concerning the nature and severity of the individual's current emotional and behavioral problems. Intellectually-limited, psychotic, or borderline clients may have a limited capacity to learn and employ the disputational techniques of RET; as such, teaching them alternative approaches to cognitive control—such as the use of rational self-statements—may prove to be more appropriate. Ellis will frequently review the client's Biographical Information Form at the start of an initial session, and will request further information to supplement that which is contained within it.

As stated in Chapter 1, irrational beliefs are viewed as the major determinants of emotional disturbance and dysfunctional behavior; hence, their identification represents the central diagnostic task for Ellis and other rational-emotive therapists. Considering that Ellis is the creator of RET and has had nearly four decades of experience in helping clients to uncover their patterns of faulty thinking, it is hardly surprising that he is remarkably adept at doing this. Usually before his first session with a new client is even half over, he has advanced a number of hypotheses concerning the cognitive factors that are largely responsible for the individual's current problems in living. These hypotheses are expressed aloud, for two major reasons: They serve as a means for teaching the client the relationship between thoughts and feelings, and they provide an opportunity for Ellis to gauge the accuracy of his clinical hunches through observation of the client's subsequent responses within the session. This second reason has particular relevance for the process of rational-emotive diagnosis, as Ellis will not hesitate to reject a hypothesis when presented with sufficient evidence of its invalidity. When a hunch proves to be inaccurate, he will simply continue the process of listening, observing, and advancing hypotheses until he is reasonably certain that he is on target.

How does Ellis manage to identify a given client's musts, shoulds, and have tos so quickly? Generally, he seems to listen for indications as to the particular types of emotional upsets the client is experiencing, and then utilizes rational-emotive theory to draw inferences regarding the types of irrational beliefs that could lie behind them. Thus, for example, he will immediately speculate that the apparently angry client is holding rigid demands regarding the manner in which other people *should* behave, while the anxious client is maintaining the belief that certain anticipated events are awful and therefore *must* not occur. This procedure is not always as straightforward as it might at first appear, as clients do not always explicitly label their affective experiences. Instead, they will frequently describe the

Date _____

mo.   day   yr.

Name _____

(last)   (first)   (middle)

Consultation Center

Institute for Rational-Emotive Therapy

45 East 65th Street ● New York, N. Y. 10021

Biographical Information Form

Instructions To assist us in helping you, please fill out this form as frankly as you can. You will save much time and effort by giving us full information. You can be sure that, like everything you say at the Institute, the facts on this form will be held in the strictest confidence and that no outsider will be permitted to see your case record without your written permission. PLEASE TYPE OR PRINT YOUR ANSWERS.

1. Date of birth: _____ Age: _____ Sex: M____ . F_____
                mo.   day   yr.

2. Address: _____
               street   city   state   zip

3. Home phone: _____ Business phone: _____

4. Permanent address **(if different from above)** _____

_____

_____

5. Who referred you to the Institute? **(check one)**

    _____(1) self _____(2) school or teacher _____(3) psychologist or psychiatrist _____(4) social agency _____(5) hospital or clinic _____(6) family doctor _____(7) friend _____(8) relative _____(9) other (explain) _____

    Has this party been here? _____Yes _____No

6. Present marital status:

    _____(1) never married _____(2) married now for first time _____(3) married now for second (or more) time

    _____(4) separated _____(5) divorced and not remarried _____(6) widowed and not remarried

    Number of years married to present spouse _____ Ages of male children _____ Ages of female children _____

7. Years of formal education completed (circle number of years):

    1 2 3 4 5 6 7 8 9 10 11 12 13 14 15 16 17 18 19 20   more than 20

8. How religious are you? **(circle number on scale that best approximates your degree of religiosity):**

    very   average   atheist
    1 2 3 4 5 6 7 8 9

9. Mother's age: _____If deceased, how old were you when she died? _____

10. Father's age: _____If deceased, how old were you when he died? _____

11. If your mother and father separated, how old were you at the time? _____

12. If your mother and father divorced, how old were you at the time? _____

13. Total number of times mother divorced _____ Number of times father divorced _____

14. Number of living brothers _____ Number of living sisters _____

TABLE 2.1 Biographical Information Form

15. Ages of living brothers _____   Ages of living sisters _____

16. I was child number _____ in a family of _____ children.

17. Were you adopted?   _____Yes   _____No

18. What kind of treatment have you previously had for emotional problems?

_____ hours of individual therapy, spread over _____ years, ending _____ years ago.

19. Hours of group therapy _____   Months of psychiatric hospitalization _____

20. Are you undergoing treatment anywhere else now? _____Yes   _____No

21. Number of times during past year you have taken antidepressants _____

22. Type of psychotherapy you have mainly had **(briefly describe method of treatment—ex., dream analysis, free association**

drugs, hypnosis, etc.) _____

_____

23. Briefly list (PRINT) your present main complaints, symptoms, and problems:_____

_____

_____

_____

24. Briefly list any additional **past** complaints, symptoms, and problems: _____

_____

_____

25. Under what conditions are your problems worse? _____

_____

_____

26. Under what conditions are they improved?_____

_____

_____

27. List the things you like to do most, the kinds of things and persons that give you pleasure:_____

_____

_____

28. List your main assets and good points: _____

_____

_____

TABLE 2.1 (continued)

29. List your main bad points: _____

_____

_____

_____

30. List your main **social** difficulties: _____

_____

_____

31. List your main **love and sex** difficulties: _____

_____

_____

32. List your main **school or work** difficulties: _____

_____

_____

33. List your main life goals: _____

_____

_____

34. List the things about yourself you would most like to change: _____

_____

_____

35. List your chief physical ailments, diseases, complaints, or handicaps: _____

_____

_____

36. What occupation(s) have you mainly been trained for? _____

    Present occupation _____ _____Full time _____Part time

37. Spouse's occupation _____ _____Full time _____Part time

38. Mother's occupation _____ Father's occupation _____

39. Mother's religion _____ Father's religion _____

40. If your mother and father did not raise you when you were young, who did? _____

TABLE 2.1 (continued)

41. Briefly describe the type of person your mother (or stepmother or person who substituted for your mother) was when you were a child and how you got along with her: _____

_____

_____

42. Briefly describe the type of person your father (or stepfather or father substitute) was when you were a child and how you got along with him: _____

_____

_____

43. If there were unusually disturbing features in your relationship to any of your brothers, briefly describe: _____

_____

_____

44. If there were unusually disturbing features in your relationship to any of your sisters, briefly describe: _____

_____

_____

45. Number of close male relatives who have been seriously emotionally disturbed: _____ Number that have been hospitalized for psychiatric treatment, or have attempted suicide: _____ Number of close female relatives who have been seriously emotionally disturbed: _____ Number that have been hospitalized for psychiatric treatment. or have attempted suicide: _____

46. Additional information that you think might be helpful

_____

_____

_____

_____

_____

_____

_____

_____

_____

_____

TABLE 2.1 (continued)

situations and events they associate with their upsets, or make reference to troubling excesses or deficits in their behavior. In either case, Ellis draws upon his years of clinical experience (as well as upon RET theory) to deduce the inappropriate negative emotion which will lead him on the trail of the client's primary irrational beliefs. He has learned that human beings characteristically feel certain emotions in connection with particular types of activating events, and that specific emotional states typically precede instances of dysfunctional behavior.

When presenting clients with his hypotheses concerning their major irrational beliefs, Ellis employs a style that is straightforward and easy to understand. He avoids using professional jargon and overly technical explanations, thus making his messages accessible to even the most psychologically unsophisticated individuals. The following brief excerpt, drawn from a session with a 38-year-old male suffering from impotence and performance anxiety, can be considered illustrative:

> ELLIS: The way to get at your interfering thoughts is to look for the *should*, whenever you experience an upset. Can you see what your shoulds are in this case? You have two or three of them.
>
> CLIENT: Not quite, no.
>
> ELLIS: Well, you can almost always see them in operation with respect to some kind of perceived failure. "I *should* be succeeding! I *should* have the love of my wife! I *should* be able to perform better than the other guy!" Aren't they there?
>
> CLIENT: Yes—I suppose that's true.
>
> ELLIS: Well, what are you doing to contradict them, to dispute them?
>
> CLIENT: I'm just falling prey to them, I think.
>
> ELLIS: At this point you're not finding the shoulds, which as I said are almost always there! "I *must* succeed, I *should* succeed, I've *got to* succeed!" You're not finding them, because I don't think you're looking for them. And, you're not disputing them, contradicting them, questioning them. Therefore they'll always return to smite you, as long as they remain a part of your basic philosophy.

In this passage it can be seen that Ellis doesn't make use of the term "irrational beliefs"; rather, he makes reference to the individual's shoulds, musts, and have tos. After first checking to see whether the client is able to identify his interfering thoughts, Ellis offers his own hypotheses and then seeks agreement from the client as to their validity. Finally, he shows the client that it is possible to use both emotional upsets and self-defeating behavior as cues to the identification of absolutistic demands. During the portion of the session immediately following this excerpt, Ellis continues the process of teaching the client the means for disputing his irrational beliefs.

PROVIDING CLIENTS WITH AN IMMEDIATE SENSE OF RELIEF AND HOPE

Ellis (1980b) believes that truly effective psychotherapy possesses a quality which he has termed *pervasiveness*. By his definition, pervasiveness in therapy means that the therapist not only assists clients in overcoming their most immediate presenting symptoms, but also attempts to equip them with the tools necessary to alleviate serious emotional upsets long after therapy has ended. Along with this focus on enduring and generalized treatment effects, Ellis's approach to therapy has the potential to leave clients feeling considerably less distressed even after their very first session. He accomplishes this feat through the following mechanisms:

Defining and Circumscribing the Client's Problems

When clients first present themselves for psychotherapy, they are sometimes confused as to the precise nature of their difficulties. By employing the ABC model in either explicit or implied form, Ellis is able to teach them that their problems can be defined in terms of the emotional and behavioral consequences of maintaining particular irrational beliefs. Although understanding this relationship is not sufficient to produce long-lasting change, it can serve to show clients that it is possible to bring some degree of order to the psychological chaos which they might be experiencing.

Helping Clients to Overcome Feelings of Hopelessness

Even when clients are able to untangle the disorder they perceive their lives to be in, they may cause themselves to feel overwhelmed by the number and severity of their emotional and behavioral problems. Lacking hope that they will be able to resolve their difficulties, they may decide that their burdens are simply "too much" to bear. Ellis effectively inspires hope in clients by showing them that a step-by-step approach to emotional problem-solving can be the best approach to making therapeutic gains. He presents them with techniques for alleviating their distress, and emphasizes that they can learn to employ these interventions without becoming dependent upon a therapist. While he stresses that progress will result mainly from continued and concentrated effort, he offers encouragement regarding the client's ability to undertake the task.

Identifying and Disputing the Client's Irrational Beliefs

As stated above, teaching clients the relationship between their irrational beliefs and emotional disturbance helps them to define and circumscribe their problems. In addition to showing them the thoughts that produce their upsets, Ellis also generally tries to conduct in-session disputation during his initial meetings with clients. By vigorously employing logical arguments, he is sometimes able to make some headway in terms of demonstrating the fallacious nature of their absolutistic demands. Relief from emotional distress can occur as clients become better able to consider alternative ways of viewing the activating events with which they are confronted.

Assisting Clients with Second-Order Problems

When clients apply irrational philosophies to their perceptions of their primary emotional difficulties, they are likely to experience second-order problems. As an example, it is frequently the case that clients will engage in considerable negative self-evaluation when they see that they are upset and not handling things as well as they think they must. Ellis is very sensitive to these "problems about problems," as he believes that it is often good practice to first work toward their alleviation before attempting to intervene with the client's primary emotional problems. After clients are somewhat freed from the extra stress produced by negative self-evaluation, they are able to stop questioning their worth and competence. This, in turn, allows them to more fully face their primary problems and more effectively dispute their irrational beliefs.

Giving the Initial Homework Assignment

Toward the end of the first session, Ellis almost invariably instructs his clients to read some of his self-help materials prior to their next scheduled appointment. While this directive will not necessarily contribute to a sense of relief in and of itself, it can be considered a component of Ellis's message that it is possible to overcome one's presenting complaints through independent action. With this emphasis upon independent action, clients can help themselves to gain a greater sense of control over their therapy and their problems.

It should be noted that providing clients with a sense of relief during their first session can present distinct drawbacks as well as advantages. In some cases, clients who "feel better" after seeing Ellis may decide that there is no need to pursue further therapy. Thus, they lose the opportunity to work at effecting the deep-seated philosophical changes that will help them to cope with future significant upsets. While Ellis usually doesn't appear to explicitly advise clients against premature termination, he does strongly imply that meaningful change requires strong and continued effort. Clients who understand and accept this communication are probably more likely to remain in treatment until they reach the point where they can act "as their own therapist."

NOTES

1. Ellis (1989) estimates that approximately 30% of his clients are influenced by his prominence in the field of psychotherapy.

3

Providing an Emotional Education: Teaching the Basic ABC's of RET

I take a very active-directive role as a psychotherapist. My main activity, most of the time, consists of involved, concerned, vigorous *teaching*. (Ellis, 1973a, p. 15)

Rational-emotive therapy (RET) is a distinctly psycho-educational approach to helping individuals overcome their emotional disturbance and dysfunctional behavior. As noted in Chapter 1, RET teaches clients a model for understanding how they make themselves psychologically disturbed, as well as a set of skills that they can use to combat these disturbances. Because of RET's emphasis upon the educative aspects of psychotherapy, Ellis and other rational-emotive therapists generally acknowledge the fact that one of their primary roles within therapy sessions is that of an authoritative (though not authoritarian) teacher.

While it is true that RET has a strong educational focus, it should be noted that "good" RET consists of considerably more than providing the client with a cut-and-dried presentation of rational-emotive principles. Indeed, it is doubtful that most clients would be receptive and responsive to a therapist who merely lectured them (albeit on a one-to-one basis) on the emotional "facts of life." In order to be maximally effective in helping their clients, rational-emotive therapists employ many of the same strategies and techniques utilized within other modes of therapy. Thus, in addition to being didactic and confrontative, they may make use of Rogerian-style reflective statements, self-disclosure, modeling, and a host of other techniques and strategies that stem from other psychotherapeutic schools. Ideally, efforts are made to establish a therapeutic relationship in which client and therapist are both active collaborators in the task of helping the client to approach his or her psychotherapeutic goals. In this vein, RET can best be described as a technically eclectic (but theoretically consistent) approach to psychotherapy (Dryden, 1986a).

Conveying the ABC model to clients represents one of the most important teaching tasks of the rational-emotive therapist. As outlined in Chapter 1, the "A" in the ABC model stands for Activating Event. An Activating Event can consist of environmental conditions or happenings which the individual finds aversive; it can also consist primarily of internal experiences, such as particular thoughts or emotions. "B" stands for Beliefs: The individual's rational and irrational cognitions concerning the Activating Event. Rational-emotive theory views these cognitions as the main determinants of "C," which denotes the individual's Consequent Emotions and Behaviors. Rational beliefs will most often result in facilitative and appropriate (although perhaps still negative) emotions at "C," with accompanying rational, self-enhancing behaviors. Irrational beliefs will most often result in disruptive and inappropriate Emotional Consequences, and will contribute to irrational, self-defeating behaviors. Thus, modification of belief systems (through cognitive, emotive, and behavioral means) is held by RET to represent the most effective and efficient vehicle for altering potentially self-destructive patterns of feeling and acting.[1]

Learning the ABC model provides several potential benefits to clients. First, when the concepts comprising this model are conveyed in an effective fashion, they represent a "common language" which can be employed by both therapist and client. When these two individuals utilize a shared vocabulary within therapy sessions, opportunities for misunderstandings are decreased and communication is facilitated.[2] In addition, the ABC model can assist clients in feeling more hopeful about the possibility of overcoming their presenting problems. It gives them a structured means for analyzing their emotional and behavioral disturbances, which can help them to make sense of an otherwise confusing array of dysfunctional thoughts, feelings, and actions. It shows them that they are not the victims of their past history or current circumstances, and illustrates the fact that the "cause" of their disturbance is a factor over which they can exercise (if they so choose) a considerable degree of control.

Within therapy sessions, the ABC model can be conveyed both directly and indirectly. On some occasions with particular clients, it makes sense for the therapist to make a highly didactic presentation of the model, with A, B, and C being explicitly defined and described.[3] While it is not Ellis's approach, some rational-emotive therapists occasionally find it helpful to draw for clients a diagram that illustrates the relationships between the model's three primary components. In terms of indirect teaching of the model, there are times when it is more appropriate to subject the client's reports of his or her experiences to an ABC analysis without explicitly employing terms such as "Activating Event" or "Consequent Emotions." As an example of this, the following exchange could occur between a client and a therapist during an initial session:

THERAPIST: What's the main problem you would like to work on right now?
CLIENT: Well, my boss is driving me crazy!
(The client's response appears to make reference to a disturbing Consequent Emotion, and hints at his belief that external circumstances are responsible for it.)
THERAPIST: Can you give me a recent example of what you mean?
(A more detailed description of a relevant Activating Event is elicited.)
CLIENT: She places all kinds of unreasonable demands on me! There's just no satisfying her! Just this past week, she gave me a major project to work on—and told me it had to be completed in just two days! Boy, I was really boiling!
THERAPIST: So you were really angry!
(The therapist is fairly certain that the client is referring primarily to feelings of anger, but uses this statement to check her perception.)
CLIENT: That's an understatement. I was enraged!
THERAPIST: Because you were telling yourself . . . what?
(The therapist asks a question in order to determine the client's Beliefs regarding his boss' behavior.)
CLIENT: She has *no right* to do that! It's totally unreasonable, and she's putting me in a very difficult position!
THERAPIST: . . . as she *must* not?
(The therapist has formed tentative hypotheses about the irrational beliefs to which the client subscribes, and attempts to test their validity with this second question.)
CLIENT: That's right! How can anyone in a position of authority act in such a stupid way?

This session could continue with the therapist providing explanations as to the distinction between preferences and demands, and the role of irrational beliefs in producing feelings of anger and other inappropriate negative emotions. As can be seen, however, this illustrative vignette touches upon all of the elements of an ABC analysis, without making specific reference to the terminology employed within the model. Through repeated exposure to these types of exchanges, clients can eventually learn to examine the relationship between their Beliefs and Consequent Emotions and Behaviors without the presence of a guiding therapist. They are then in a position to independently identify and dispute their upset-producing irrational beliefs.

It should be noted that the ABC model contains certain nuances which are not necessarily conveyed by teaching the terms Activating Event, Beliefs, and Consequent Emotions and Behaviors. In order for the model to be optimally useful to clients as a tool for combatting their upsets, it is also desirable that they learn how to:

1. Access their affect-producing thoughts independently, and make the distinction between thoughts and feelings,
2. Recognize that "A" doesn't cause "C"; rather, "B" mainly causes "C,"
3. Distinguish between rational and irrational beliefs, and accurately identify their operative irrational beliefs,
4. Understand the distinctions between appropriate and inappropriate negative emotions, and
5. Understand the relationship between primary and second-order emotional problems.

The sections that follow will elaborate on the importance of each of these psycho-educational "units," and will offer descriptions of the manner in which Ellis conveys them to clients. As will be the case for most of the chapters comprising this book, excerpts derived from audiotapes of Ellis's sessions will be employed for purposes of illustration.

HELPING CLIENTS TO ACCESS AFFECT-PRODUCING THOUGHTS

During the course of a typical session, Ellis will employ various types of accessing questions in order to elicit clients' upset-producing irrational beliefs. Ellis will show clients how these irrational beliefs result in inappropriate negative emotions, and will then set about the business of disputing and attempting to replace them with more rational (and functional) alternative beliefs. Over the course of several sessions, clients learn that they can ask themselves these same sorts of questions and independently access the cognitions which contribute to their feelings of anxiety, depression, guilt, shame, and anger.

With newer clients, the process of eliciting irrational beliefs is not always entirely straightforward. Such clients are often not accustomed to being asked to examine their thinking, and will often respond to Ellis's accessing questions by reporting their perceptions or inferences regarding a particular

Activating Event. While these perceptions and inferences may themselves represent faulty thinking, they are regarded as being the by-products of irrational beliefs (DiGiuseppe, 1986; Dryden & Ellis, 1987). As such, Ellis generally devotes little time to disputing them. Instead, he will continue his line of questioning in order to uncover the musts and shoulds which lie behind and perhaps cause these inaccurate perceptions and inferences. The following excerpt, drawn from the beginning of a session with a young, socially anxious male, illustrates this questioning process:

> ELLIS: What's doing with you?
> CLIENT: Oh, the same old shit.
> ELLIS: Well, give me an example. Tell me something specific that you've been bothering yourself about, and we'll examine it.
> CLIENT: O.K. . . . Well, for instance, this week my supervisor called me into his office so that he could introduce me to two new business associates. I get very nervous during these introductions . . .
> ELLIS: Because you tell yourself what?
> CLIENT: Well, I wonder what they're going to think about me. I worry about the kind of impression I'm making.
> ELLIS: Let's suppose you make a *bad* impression—let's just suppose that. *Then* what do you tell yourself?
> CLIENT: That it's my fault, that I've failed . . .
> ELLIS: ". . . and I'm a failure." Right?
> CLIENT: Right.
> ELLIS: Now, let's assume that in this case you did fail—although we don't even know that that's true. How does that make you a failure?

In this excerpt, the client responds to Ellis's original accessing question by making reference to his worries about leaving a good impression with his business associates. Given the fact that this is only his second session, it is not surprising that he fails to verbalize concisely the particular irrational belief which underlies his interpersonal anxiety. Seeing this, Ellis continues his questions until he manages to uncover the negative self-rating process in which the client engages. The session continues with Ellis showing him the fallacious nature of his negative self-evaluations, and how he subscribes to the idea that "I *must* have the approval of those whom I consider significant in order to be a worthwhile person."

With more sophisticated clients (i.e., those who have acquired some knowledge regarding the nature of irrational beliefs), Ellis will often employ more direct types of accessing questions. In the following exchange, Ellis utilizes this approach with a depressed middle-aged woman who has previously provided herself with a grounding in rational-emotive theory by reading suggested books and pamphlets:

CLIENT: This past week I thought about all of the problems that I have, and I got myself very depressed. I said to myself, "My God, when am I ever going to change?"

ELLIS: Do you see the must that you have in there?

CLIENT: Yes—I've got to get myself better right away.

ELLIS: That's right. Also, it sounds like you're saying, "I must not have so many problems." You see, you even sneak in musts about the therapy! If you said, "I *wish* I didn't have all of these problems—but I do—now let me work on them without demanding immediate changes," then you wouldn't get yourself depressed about your problems.

As this client is already able to recognize the relationship between her irrational beliefs and depressed moods, Ellis does not employ the more general "What were you telling yourself?" line of questioning. Instead, he asks her to try to identify the specific demand behind her upset, and elaborates upon her response. Aside from illustrating Ellis's use of more direct accessing questions, this excerpt is noteworthy in that it provides an example of how Ellis will direct attention to clients' thoughts and feelings about the therapeutic process. By bringing to the fore this particular client's irrational beliefs about her therapy, he is able to help her avoid the potential pitfalls of low frustration tolerance and negative self-evaluation.

On occasion, some of Ellis's clients will make reference to having a particular type of emotional problem, but will be vague as to the Activating Events which tend to trigger it. In such situations, Ellis will sometimes invent a hypothetical Activating Event to serve as a vehicle for assessing the client's self-defeating cognitions. In the following example, he uses this tactic with a young woman who reports that she is too shy to approach and speak to men in any but the most structured social situations:

ELLIS: Let's suppose that you're on a bank line, and there's an attractive man right next to you. You'd like to talk to him, but you don't. Now, what would you be telling yourself to stop yourself from talking to him? You're telling yourself something—do you realize what it is? "If I talk to him . . . ," what?

CLIENT: He may ask me out, and then I'll be put on the line, I guess.

ELLIS: But let's suppose that's the case. You talk to him and he asks you out. What would be bad about that?

CLIENT: Nothing, except that I would get very nervous. I came from a very strict background . . .

ELLIS: Well, don't blame it on your background—you're bright enough to get over your goddamn background!

CLIENT: I didn't start dating 'till I was in college—I still feel like a novice!

ELLIS: So you didn't start dating at age 10, like the rest of us did!

CLIENT: (Laughs.)

ELLIS: There's still something you're afraid of. Now, what would you be telling yourself to make yourself anxious?

CLIENT: I might get stage-fright.

ELLIS: Yes, but stage-fright means, "I'm going to say something stupid or wrong, and that would be awful!" You're perfectionistic, you see. You're demanding a scenario in which you say exactly the right things, and you go out with him and *do* exactly the right things, and then the two of you walk off into the sunset together. But that's not going to be! Nobody is that perfect! Now, why do you *have* to be? What's he going to do when he finds out you don't do everything perfectly—run away vomiting, or what?

In this example, it is apparent that the client does not respond to Ellis's accessing questions by immediately relating her self-talk about the hypothetical Activating Event. It is important to note, however, that Ellis chooses not to belabor the assessment process by continuing to pepper her with questions; instead, he adopts a didactic mode and directly teaches her about the origins of stage-fright and the role played by perfectionism in producing her social reticence. By alternating between questioning and direct teaching, Ellis is able to make his therapy more efficient and can avoid jeopardizing his rapport with clients.

TEACHING CLIENTS THE B → C CONNECTION

As noted above, the ABC model holds that Activating Events may contribute to, but do not cause, specific Consequent Emotions and Behaviors. Rather, it is an individual's Beliefs about the Activating Event that largely result in particular emotional and behavioral outcomes. In abbreviated form, these relationships can be expressed as follows: A $\nrightarrow$ C; B → C (translation: "A" doesn't cause "C"; "B" mainly causes "C").

These relationships are, of course, the basic premises of the ABC model. As such, it is important for clients to acknowledge and understand them early on in their therapy. Ellis can be quite vociferous in his attempts to teach clients that A $\nrightarrow$ C, particularly when they refer to their early experiences as the source of their current difficulties. Here, he tries to put this notion to rest during his first session with a young male client:

Emotional disturbance doesn't come from anybody's fucking childhood. The idea that your mother made you disturbed is Freudian horseshit! The Freudians always forget to ask the most relevant question: "Who listened to your mother's crap?" The answer is, "You did!" And who carried on her slop to the present day? Again, the answer is, "You did!" As Pogo said, "We have met the enemy, and it is us!" We upset *ourselves*! Nobody in human history was ever *made* upset.

To a client who is blaming her current upsets upon the stressors confronting her at work, Ellis makes the following response:

The job is difficult right now, and your boss may tend to be unreasonable. That's the way it is. You can look for another job, but while you're still there the point is to stop stressing *yourself*. You're taking circumstances *too* seriously, and that's where your stress comes from. It doesn't *just* come from the situation.

During a first session with a young female who experiences panic attacks, Ellis devotes considerable time to highlighting the B → C connection. He begins by taking a highly didactic approach, perhaps because the client appears to be lacking in insights as to the "cause" of her problems:

Your anxiety is caused by two demands: Number one, that "I must do well," and number two, that "I must get other people to approve of me." Under certain conditions—such as when you go for job interviews—you get yourself anxious. Now, why *must* you do well? I'm not asking you why it would be preferable to do well, but why you *have* to.

Later in the session, Ellis adopts a more interactive approach in order to "test" this client's understanding of the role played by her irrational beliefs in producing her anxiety:

ELLIS: Your problem is to see that everytime you get anxious, you've got a must. Give me a recent example of a time when you were anxious.
CLIENT: Well, I was up in Massachusetts looking for a job . . .
ELLIS: And you were anxious during the interview?
CLIENT: Yes.
ELLIS: All right, do you see your must? "I must . . . ," what?
CLIENT: I must get the job.
ELLIS: That's right! Why do you *have* to? It would be lovely, great, and desirable—we're not putting it down—but you don't *have* to. Give me another instance recently when you were anxious—about anything.
CLIENT: I went to a party with some friends.
ELLIS: O.K., what was your must then?
CLIENT: I must be happy and laugh with everyone . . .
ELLIS: "I must impress them." *Why* must you?
CLIENT: I don't fit in; I'm not normal.
ELLIS: Why *must* you show them that you're normal?
CLIENT: There's no reason!

ELLIS: That's right! But you see, you'd better *practice* that line of thinking: "There's no goddamn reason why I must!"

The importance of teaching clients that A $\nrightarrow$ C; B $\rightarrow$ C should not be underestimated, as this insight is one of the cornerstones of RET. If clients fail to understand these relationships or resist acknowledging their validity, then they may be prone to blame their present emotional and behavioral disturbances upon their childhood experiences (or other aspects of their prior histories) and current environmental conditions. Such misattributions make it much less likely that clients will assume responsibility for working to overcome their problems. As a result, it is probable that they will make minimal (if any) progress within their therapy.

TEACHING THE DIFFERENCE BETWEEN RATIONAL AND IRRATIONAL BELIEFS

RET teaches clients to distinguish between their rational and irrational beliefs, in order that they might become able to identify independently the thinking that lies behind their upsets. Ellis (and other RET practitioners) often present this distinction by highlighting the difference between needs and wants. Within the RET framework, individuals create "needs" when they elevate their basic wants, preferences, and desires into absolute musts. In the excerpt that follows, Ellis explains this distinction to a client who complains that she is unable to overcome her compulsive eating habits:

ELLIS: . . . You're telling yourself, "Because I want the food, I *must* have it!" Well, does that logically follow?
CLIENT: No.
ELLIS: That's right. Now, if you rip that up many times and show yourself that no matter how much you want the extra food, you *never* have to have it, you'll solve your problem. I'm not asking you why you want it—you want it because it tastes good and it's pleasurable. But, you don't *need* what you *want*! There are no absolute musts in the universe—they simply don't exist!

In terms of teaching clients to identify their operative irrational beliefs, Ellis will make statements such as this: "It's very simple to learn how to find your irrational beliefs, because they all seem to have musts in them. Whenever you're depressed, anxious, or ashamed, look for your must!"

In this next exchange, Ellis employs an approach that is intended to prompt the client to identify for himself the source of his anxiety:

ELLIS: At "A" you had an important business meeting to attend, and at "C" you felt very anxious. Is that correct?

CLIENT: That's correct.

ELLIS: All right—I already know what "B" is. How do you think I know? I've only seen you for a few minutes, and I don't know that much about you, but I know what your "B" is. Do you know why I know it?

CLIENT: Because I'm a classic case of a nutjob?

ELLIS: Because I asked myself, "What *must* is he telling himself? He can't get upset without a must."

CLIENT: I must be feeling anxious, I must be feeling lousy?

ELLIS: That may be part of it, but there's a particular one that you're telling yourself about your meeting. What would you be saying about the meeting to cause your anxiety?

CLIENT: I've got to . . . to impress these people.

ELLIS: Right—"I must do well!" Not, "I'd like to"—that wouldn't get you anxious. If you said, "I *wish* to, but if I don't, then fuck it," you wouldn't get anxious.

TEACHING THE DISTINCTION BETWEEN APPROPRIATE AND INAPPROPRIATE NEGATIVE EMOTIONS

One of the central goals of RET is to help clients learn to overcome their feelings of depression, guilt, anger, anxiety, and shame. Within the RET framework, these affective states are usually referred to as inappropriate negative emotions. While it is readily apparent that they are all negative in nature, they are deemed inappropriate because they stem from irrational thinking and interfere with an individual's ability to take pleasure in life and pursue important goals.

It is critical to note, however, that RET does *not* seek to assist individuals in overcoming *all* negative emotional experiences. This is because, in Ellis's view, a rationally-thinking person will still have negative feelings when blocked from attaining significant (as defined by the individual) desires and preferences. These feelings—which include such states as sadness, regret, annoyance, and frustration—are labelled appropriate negative emotions, as they represent a more reality-based response to unfortunate or undesirable circumstances. They are considered to be facilitative feelings, in the sense that they will motivate an individual to work at changing modifiable features of his or her environment and adjust constructively to those features that cannot be modified. Thus, from a long-term perspective, appropriate negative emotions can function to enhance a person's productivity and enjoyment of life.

On occasion, Ellis will make a special point of reviewing the distinction between appropriate and inappropriate emotions with clients.[4] In the exchange that follows, he explains this distinction to a young female client whose lover has recently ended their relationship:

CLIENT: How am I supposed to stop missing him?

ELLIS: Oh no, you *will* miss him for the time being. When you don't get what you want, you feel loss, or regret, or sorrow, or frustration. Right now, you're going to feel frustrated—but you don't *have* to feel hung-up and horrified. You have a hassle, a big hassle—so we're not minimizing it— but a hassle is not a fucking horror! Even with things being the way they are now, you could continue to live and be a happy human.

As far as your relationship with him is concerned, you're not getting what you want. So, there's no way that you can be un-sad and un-frustrated. Sadness and frustration are unpleasant, but they're *good* emotions. They'll motivate you to try and get back with him, or to seek a relationship with somebody else. There's nothing wrong with that!

We don't want you to feel good or overjoyed about it: "Oh goody-goody, I lost the bastard!" That would be nonsense! You'd better feel sorry and sad, and at times even cry out of *sorrow*—but not out of depression. When you're depressed, it's because you're saying, "Woe is me, I can't stand it! I need what I want, and the world has nothing in it for me if I can't have this piece of taffy." That's where your depression comes from.

Clients who fail to understand that RET will not help them do away with their appropriate negative emotions may set unreasonable therapeutic goals for themselves, such as attempting to have only positive affective experiences or to feel neutral in response to negative Activating Events. They are quite likely to be disappointed in their efforts, which could lead them to erroneously conclude that their therapy is proving ineffective. As such, it is quite important for them to learn this distinction.

TEACHING THE RELATIONSHIP BETWEEN PRIMARY AND SECONDARY EMOTIONAL PROBLEMS

RET recognizes the fact that individuals can create second-order emotional problems by disturbing themselves about their original presenting symptoms. In order to illustrate this process, consider the hypothetical case example of a woman who enters therapy because of her concern over her frequent angry outbursts at her husband and child. As her therapist begins to work with her, it might become apparent that she not only has the original presenting problem of anger, but that she also has a secondary emotional problem: Guilt. According to the ABC model, her primary and secondary disturbances could be conceptualized as follows:

A 1: Husband and/or child behave in ways which client perceives as inconsiderate.

B 1: "They *shouldn't* act in such inconsiderate ways; they *should* appreciate all that I do for them! They're ungrateful louses!"

C 1: Anger, accompanied by rageful behavior.

A 2: Client's perceptions regarding her own anger and rageful behavior.

B 2: "*I shouldn't* lose my temper with them; I'm a failure."

C 2: Guilt, accompanied by inappropriate conciliatory behavior.

As can be seen in this sequence, the client's primary "C" (anger) becomes a new (or secondary) "A." By applying a second set of irrational beliefs to this new "A," she makes herself feel guilty over the fact that she becomes angry. Just as this client creates a specific second-order symptom for herself, it is conceivable that other individuals could make themselves anxious about their anxiety, ashamed about their depression, and so on.

Unlike many other currently practiced forms of psychotherapy, RET places a unique emphasis upon such secondary emotional problems (Ellis & Bernard, 1985). Rational-emotive therapists are generally trained to address these second-order disturbances first, prior to focusing upon remediation of the client's original symptom. In the following excerpt, Ellis explains the genesis of second-order problems to a highly anxious female client:

ELLIS: Let's go through the ABC's of your problems very clearly. First, you have your original issue: "If I screw up at work, I'm a shit." "A" is the Activating Event of having to complete some task at work. "B" is, "I must not screw up, I must do a great job and make a good impression on the boss." Then "C" is anxiety. Right?

CLIENT: That sounds right.

ELLIS: Now you take "C"—your anxiety—and you make it into a new "A"! At "B," you say to yourself, "I must not be anxious—that would be awful!" Then "C" becomes anxiety about anxiety! You see, you produce a secondary symptom by doing the same thing on two levels. Now, we want to undo those two symptoms, so we'll start with the secondary anxiety. Why *must* you not be anxious?

The session proceeds with Ellis continuing to focus upon the client's second-order anxiety. Once she is able to understand the manner in which she produces this additional upset, he switches his focus back to her original set of musts concerning her work performance. It is noted that the above excerpt is somewhat unusual, in that Ellis does not often explain secondary problems to clients by specifically outlining how they fit into the ABC format. Nevertheless, review of his audiotapes suggests that he is quite sensitive with regard to identifying such problems and attacking the irrational beliefs which produce them. This is of considerable importance in

RET, as second-order disturbances can represent a significant obstacle to a client's overcoming original presenting complaints.

CLOSING COMMENTS

In introducing one of the excerpts presented above, it was mentioned that the client had provided herself with a foundation in RET by completing assigned readings (see pp. 38–39). Bibliotherapy represents another vehicle for conveying the ABC model to clients, and is frequently utilized by Ellis and other practitioners of RET. As such, clients who enter therapy at the Institute for Rational-Emotive Therapy in New York City are provided with a free packet of pamphlets which provide a general explication of rational-emotive theory, as well as a description of the manner in which RET can be applied to a host of possible presenting problems. Clients who complete this reading material provide themselves with a distinct advantage in therapy, as they are better able to "catch on" to the approach their therapist employs with them during therapy sessions. Thus, their RET will tend to proceed in a more effective and efficient fashion.

Within RET, a client's emotional education does not end with the teaching of the ABC's. Strictly speaking, the ABC's can provide insights as to the *source* of dysfunctional emotions and behaviors, but do not in and of themselves provide the key to *overcoming* these obstacles to happiness and goal-attainment. In order to acquire the skills necessary to accomplish this end, they must also learn the "D" and "E" of the ABC model: Disputing irrational beliefs in order to achieve a more rational philosphical Effect. The next chapter will describe Ellis's approach to teaching clients the skills involved in disputation.

NOTES

1. It is noted that Ellis (1985b) has acknowledged that emotional disturbance is not caused *solely* by irrational beliefs. Rather, he takes the position that there is significant overlap and interaction between cognition, emotion, and behavior, and that these three entities do not exist in isolation from one another. Thus, certain irrational beliefs may contribute to an individual's depression, but that person's depressive state (which may have physiological as well as psychological aspects) will also affect the nature of his or her cognitions and behaviors.

2. A number of rational-emotive therapists have written of the importance of making sure that client and therapist are using terms and phrases in the same way. Dryden (1986b), for example, has pointed out that when

clients report they are anxious about some future event, they may really mean that they're merely concerned. The therapist who neglects to check the manner in which the client is using the word "anxious" may incorrectly assume that the individual is reporting a significant emotional problem.

3. Such a mode of presentation would be appropriate with clients who learn best under highly structured conditions. Intellectually-limited or cognitively unfocused individuals could fall into this category.

4. RET also draws a distinction between appropriate and inappropriate *positive* emotions. Like inappropriate negative emotions, inappropriate positive emotions are viewed as resulting from irrational thinking. They would include such potentially self-defeating states as euphoria and grandiosity, which are often experienced during manic episodes.

4

Providing an Emotional Education: Teaching Clients How to Dispute Their Irrational Beliefs

> The central theme of RET is that human beings are uniquely rational, as well as uniquely irrational, animals; that their emotional or psychological disturbances are largely a result of their thinking illogically or irrationally, and that they can rid themselves of most of their emotional or mental unhappiness, ineffectuality, and disturbance if they learn to maximize their rational and minimize their irrational thinking. (Ellis, 1962, p. 36)

As reviewed in the preceding chapter, conveying the ABC model to clients represents one of the most important teaching tasks of the rational-emotive therapist. For clients to derive any meaningful benefit from this means for analyzing the source of their upsets, however, they must also learn how to dispute their irrational beliefs. Through the process of disputation, they can help themselves to attain a more effective, rational philosophy of life.

According to Ellis (1977a), the process of disputation includes the following components:

1. *Detecting* the irrational beliefs that lead to self-defeating emotions and behaviors.

2. *Debating* the validity of the identified irrational beliefs which appear to be operative in a given emotional episode, and
3. *Discriminating* irrational beliefs from rational beliefs, and reviewing the manner in which the former tend to lead to undesirable and the latter to more desirable emotional and behavioral consequences.

By presenting transcripts of therapy sessions with two separate clients, the current chapter will attempt to illustrate the manner in which Ellis tries to convey these three main components of disputation. The first transcript is drawn from Ellis's initial session with a client who is relatively naive regarding the principles and techniques of RET, while the second is derived from his fifth session with a very intelligent client who has managed to master the fundamentals of RET within a comparatively short span of time. In reading through these transcripts, it will become apparent that Ellis's style and approach vary in accordance with the degree of sophistication and insight which the client has attained. Clearly, he employs a different set of strategies after it has become apparent that the client is beginning to understand (and utilize) disputing techniques.

Following presentation of these two extended transcripts, a summary of the most relevant differences between Ellis's approach in earlier and later sessions will be provided. This section will also include discussion of some additional issues involved in teaching disputation skills. The chapter will conclude with a final brief excerpt which will serve as an example of the manner in which Ellis helps clients to identify and overcome obstacles to effective disputing.

AN EARLIER SESSION

The following excerpt is drawn from an initial session with a male client who has recently entered into a business venture with a reportedly unreliable partner. The business has encountered serious financial difficulties, and the client is anxious about the prospect of going bankrupt. In addition, he is angry at his partner for shirking his responsibilities, and angry at himself for not having exercised better judgment when he decided to form a partnership with this individual. During the first fifteen minutes of the session, Ellis elicits descriptions of relevant activating events, identifies the nature of the client's emotional and behavioral disturbance, and emphasizes the self-defeating aspects of his condemnation of himself and his partner. In the passage below, he reiterates this message and begins the process of teaching the client how to dispute his irrational beliefs:

CLIENT: The thought of going bankrupt has left me sleepless!
ELLIS: That's because you're worrying yourself by saying, "I shouldn't have

this partner, I must not go bankrupt, life is awful," et cetera. As long as you refuse to *accept* reality, you're not going to sleep! Reality *stinks* right now, but you'd better accept it because that's the only way you're going to be in a position to change it. The more you depress and anger yourself about it, the less energy you'll have to work at making things better. As I said before, you'd better stick your anger up your ass and live with your partner. And I don't mean suppress your anger—I mean *stop* it!

CLIENT: How do I do that?

ELLIS: By changing your philosophy and convincing yourself that people *should* be the way they are, no matter how crummy that might be. Until you really adopt a "tough shit" philosophy, you're going to be an emotional mess—and your messiness will interfere with your natural competence.

As can be seen in this excerpt, Ellis forcefully attempts to convey the notion that the client is able to exert some influence over the upsets he experiences. He makes reference to the client's personal philosophy as being responsible for these upsets, and begins to actively teach the tenets of a more rational and functional alternative philosophy.

CLIENT: I've been trying to tell myself in the last couple of days that I *will* succeed—but it's not really getting through.

ELLIS: That's called positive thinking—but I suspect that underneath, you're probably still saying, "If I don't succeed, it's awful!" You'd better say to yourself, "I'm *determined* to succeed, but even if I don't, it's only a pain in the ass. Even if this business goes bankrupt, I can still get another job and work my way up." That's the worst thing that could happen, you see.

Now, you'd better *not* say, "It *must* succeed, it *must* succeed, it *must* succeed," because there's no reason that it *has* to. It would be better if it succeeded, because that's what you want. But it doesn't *have* to, and that "must" is as harmful as saying that your partner must not be the way he is. You're *demanding* instead of desiring and working your ass off to get what you want.

CLIENT: How can I train my mind to do what you're saying?

ELLIS: By recognizing that your frame of mind is destructive, and by going over what we're discussing right now. How can your present frame of mind help you to get any of the things that you want?

CLIENT: I can see that it can't. I think I'm just so angry at myself—because I sort of saw these problems coming and I didn't pay enough attention to them.

ELLIS: But why shouldn't you make errors? You're saying, "I shouldn't have made this error, I should have known better." Now, why should you not make grave errors, like "misdiagnosing" your partner?

CLIENT: Because it's self-defeating.

ELLIS: By definition, an error is self-defeating. But why *shouldn't* you act self-defeatingly?

CLIENT: (Pause) I should listen to my instincts, and not be so stubborn.

ELLIS: That doesn't answer the question. Now, why shouldn't you act self-defeatingly? If you give a valid answer to that question, you'll start solving your problems.

Ellis identifies and labels the client's attempts to utilize "positive thinking" as a means for overcoming his upsets, and points out how his underlying irrational beliefs will serve to sabotage this approach. In addition, he Discriminates between *demanding* and *desiring*. The former is presented as creating obstacles to attaining preferred outcomes, while the latter is presented as a source of motivation for undertaking the difficult tasks with which the client is faced.

Ellis uses the client's reference to his anger at himself as a vehicle for Detecting an operative irrational belief, and then begins to actively Debate his demand that "I shouldn't act in a self-defeating manner." He provides the client with a disputing question, and underscores the importance of finding a valid answer to it.

CLIENT: On the one hand, I don't want to be a loser. But on the other hand, I've managed to get into a situation where I *am* losing. I don't know—maybe deep down I don't want to win.

ELLIS: That's psychoanalytic horseshit. The psychoanalysts are always making up nutty hypotheses like, "Maybe I don't want to win." Of course you want to! But stick to the question—don't go off into other things. "Why shouldn't I act self-defeatingly?" Now, what's the answer to that?

CLIENT: Because I've never done it before, and I can't stand people that do.

ELLIS: That's the wrong answer—now, think about it again. Until you get the answer to that question—and there's only one valid answer—you're going to be a nut for the rest of your life!

CLIENT: I can't afford that!

ELLIS: Oh, sure you can! Most people go on like that forever! But answer the question: Why *should* you not, *must* you not, act self-defeatingly?

CLIENT: I don't know . . .

ELLIS: The only answer is, "There's *no reason* why I shouldn't!" Every other answer is sheer crap! There's no reason why you *shouldn't* act self-defeatingly. There are many reasons why it's *better* not to, but that's a different issue. We're not asking why it's better—it's obvious that it's better not to act self-defeatingly. But there's no reason why you *must* not—you'll always be a fallible fucked-up human being, and I guarantee that you'll do *thousands* of stupid things for the rest of your life—and there's no reason why you shouldn't. None. Zero. Right now, you're totally non-accepting of your own fallibility. Until you accept it and say, "Yes, I've fucked up and will continue to do so for the rest of my life—tough shit, that's the way it is," you'll continue to be angry at yourself and other people. And you'll probably fuck up much more frequently.

Here, Ellis employs a Socratic questioning approach in an attempt to engage the client in the process of Debating his irrational beliefs. The client, however, distracts himself from Ellis's disputing question by speculating that he is sabotaging himself because he really lacks the desire to succeed. Ellis quickly debunks this notion, and refocuses the client to the task of examining the validity of his "must." When the client continues to provide dysfunctional responses to his question, Ellis finally provides him with the rational solution. This is done mainly for the sake of efficiency, as it has become evident that the client is quite rigid in his thinking and not yet able to recognize the alternative perspective.

CLIENT: How can I change myself?

ELLIS: By going over this ten thousand times, until you accept yourself with your fallibility. Once you accept yourself as fallible, you'll still fuck up, but you'll probably do it less often.

CLIENT: In other words, I'm entitled to make mistakes.

ELLIS: That's right! And we're not saying it's *right* to make mistakes, because it's certainly better not to—we're not denying that part. But as a fallible, screwed-up human, you'll always make many, many errors—because that's the way you are!

Now, you can train yourself to be more accepting of your own and others' fallibility. Otherwise, how can you get along competently in life if you spend so much time hating yourself and others?

CLIENT: Is there any formula?

ELLIS: This is the formula: Whenever you're upset, there's almost *always* a should or a must involved. Your two main ones are, "I must do well," and, "They must do well." Zero in on your musts when you're upset, and then ask yourself the same sort of question that I just asked you: "Why should I—or why must they—act well?" The only answer is that there's no reason why you or they *must*. Keep going through that until you really believe it.

CLIENT: Can you give me a concrete example?

ELLIS: Tell me about some specific thing that you recently got yourself upset about.

CLIENT: Well, there was some paperwork my partner was supposed to finish this afternoon—and he never touched it!

ELLIS: At "A"—that's the Activating Event—you saw that your partner was goofing. And at "C"—your Emotional Consequence—you felt angry. Right?

CLIENT: Right.

ELLIS: Now at "B"—which stands for Beliefs—you had a should or a must. Do you know what it was?

CLIENT: He should do what he's supposed to do!

ELLIS: That's right! Now, "D" stands for Disputing: Why *should* he do what he's supposed to do?

CLIENT: To help make the business successful.

ELLIS: That's why it's *preferable*! Why *should* he do what's preferable?

CLIENT: (Pause) It could make or break our company.

ELLIS: You're *still* telling me why it's preferable, and we're not disputing that! You see, you rigidly stick to the idea that because it's preferable, it *has to* be. Now, does that follow?

CLIENT: No . . .

ELLIS: So what's the answer to the question: "Why must he do what's preferable?"

CLIENT: In other words, he doesn't have to.

ELLIS: Ahhh! Now you're getting it! If you go over and over that until you really believe it, you'll change your entire emotional existence. No one *has* to do anything, no matter *how* preferable it might be—that's the way it is!

In this passage, the client begins to demonstrate some understanding of the philosophy and techniques that Ellis is trying to convey to him. He asks for a "formula" for becoming more accepting of human fallibility, and Ellis responds by giving him a concise description of the process of disputation. Ellis teaches him to use his upsets as a cue to monitor his thinking, in order that he might be able to independently identify his operative irrational beliefs. In addition, he again stresses the importance of questioning these beliefs once they have been identified, and emphasizes the idea that frequent repetition will aid in the task of cognitive modification.

When the client requests clarification of the disputing process through a "concrete example," Ellis applies an ABC analysis to one of his recent emotional episodes. When he reaches the "B" of this analysis, he asks the client to try and identify his underlying irrational belief. Although successful in his attempt, the client again provides irrelevant responses to Ellis's disputing question. After Ellis shows him that these responses represent non sequiturs, he finally manages to give a rational answer. The passage ends with Ellis reinforcing this last response with praise, and summarizing the rational alternative philosophy which it implies.

A LATER SESSION

The excerpt that follows is drawn from Ellis's fifth session with an intelligent, young male client who wishes to become more self-disciplined.

Within this session, many of the differences in the way Ellis handles disputation in earlier and later sessions will become evident. The session begins
with the client verbalizing his belief that he'll never be able to change:

ELLIS: What's happening with you?

CLIENT: I've been realizing that a lack of discipline has plagued me throughout
my life. To a certain extent I believe I'm a failure in that area, and there's
no changing that part of me.

ELLIS: Well, let's assume that you've failed and so far you haven't disciplined
yourself. How does that prove you never will?

CLIENT: It's a feeling more than a fact.

ELLIS: You'd better dispute that feeling! If you believe that you'll never change
and become more disciplined, you'll create a self-fulfilling prophecy
because you'll never try. Your feeling is really a belief—and a strong
one, at that. It serves to protect your low frustration tolerance, because
it gives you an excuse: "Well, I can't change, so what's the use of
trying?"

CLIENT: My grandfather used to tell me that a leopard can't change its spots—
and that was meant to indicate that my character was formed and there
was no improving it.

ELLIS: But you see, that view is obviously false—look at the number of people
who do well for a while and then screw up! Now, how did they change
their spots? It's very difficult to change your spots, but you're not a
leopard—you're a human being.

CLIENT: Actually, I'm satisfied with my spots—it's my behavior that I want to
change.

ELLIS: That's right—you're always going to be a human—you're not going to
change your humanity. Right now you're undisciplined and have low
frustration tolerance—but let's look at the other side for a moment. If
you *were* disciplined, what benefits would you gain?

CLIENT: Oh, tremendous benefits—I'd gain more efficient use of my time, and
the capacity to have more goal-directed types of behavior.

ELLIS: And wouldn't you lead a happi-*er* life?

CLIENT: Oh, definitely.

ELLIS: Now, that's what you're sweeping out of mind when you're undisciplined. You're focusing on the pleasures of the moment, and not the
potential for a happi-*er* life in the future. So one thing you can do is
write down all of the advantages of discipline, and all of the disadvantages of a lack of discipline, and really go over them—remind yourself
of them every day.

Here, Ellis quickly begins disputing the client's idea that it is impossible to
become more self-disciplined. He asks the client to focus on the potential
benefits of leading a more disciplined life, and describes a referenting approach
for keeping these advantages in awareness.[1] While referenting represents a

vehicle for effecting cognitive modification, Ellis typically does not introduce it during his initial sessions with clients. Rather, he tends to focus more upon introducing some of the core philosophical and technical elements of RET. Once the client demonstrates some knowledge of these elements, allied concepts and strategies (such as referenting) may be introduced.

CLIENT: Well, assuming that I were to do that . . . the thought that comes up is, "Who do you think you're kidding—why is it going to be any different *this* time?"

ELLIS: And the answer is—there's only one real answer—it *can* be different this time, with harder work. You see, it *won't* be different if (1) you have your current philosophy: "I need immediate gratification," and (2) you don't *work* at becoming more disciplined. Now, if you changed your philosophy—"I *don't* need immediate gratification; I'd rather have future gain"—and you actively pushed yourself to achieve that future gain, you'd be able to change. What makes a person change when he wants to be a better tennis player? What does he do?

CLIENT: He practices more.

ELLIS: But first he says, "I am *able* to play better, even though I haven't up 'till now," and then he pushes himself to practice, practice, practice. But he won't play better by merely *wishing* to play better (Chuckles). A large part of procrastination is the principle of inertia: It requires extra energy to get going, and then sometimes when you get started you don't want to stop. But it's uncomfortable to get going, and you're demanding in your philosophy that it be comfortable. It often won't be.

CLIENT: As you say, I have very low frustration tolerance—I get frustrated very easily.

ELLIS: Yes, but frustration doesn't amount to low frustration tolerance. The *philosophy* of low frustration tolerance is (1) "I *need* immediate ease, gratification, and comfort," and (2) "I *can't stand* immediate blocking, pain, and frustration."

CLIENT: Do you think that the only real difference in frustration levels for people is what they believe about the frustration itself?

ELLIS: No—there's one other important difference. People with high energy and enthusiasm for something tend to experience less frustration. But even those that experience *much* frustration can *push* themselves to overcome it. I often tell the story of Sinclair Lewis—he went back to Yale after he won the Nobel prize in literature, and he gave a talk on creative writing. The students said, "Well, Mr. Lewis—you're a great writer—tell us the art of writing!" And Lewis said, "It's very simple—the art of writing consists of putting the seat of the pants to the seat of the chair, and writing." And he was right!

At the beginning of this passage, the client again voices his strongly-held doubts regarding his ability to increase self-discipline. Ellis addresses this source of potential resistance by outlining the essential elements for effecting meaningful modifications in this sphere: A fundamental philosophical change concerning the "need" for immediate gratification, plus prolonged effort. In order to most effectively convey his message, he utilizes an analogy (i.e., the process of becoming a better tennis player) and a quote by a noted author. His use of this quote results in the client making reference to a specific area in which his low frustration tolerance has had a detrimental impact:

CLIENT: I'm interested in writing, but I have a difficult time getting started. And once I do get started, I have very poor stamina.

ELLIS: Let's suppose that you've gotten started—you have poor stamina because you tell yourself something at a certain point. I can guess what that might be—what do you think it is?

CLIENT: I'm not going to succeed at this, it's too difficult, I might as well not try . . .

ELLIS: All right—you see, there are two ideas in there. One is the recognition that it's become difficult: "It was easy up to this point. Now I'm stuck. It's *too* goddamn difficult—why should I do it?" The second idea is, "Since it's so difficult, maybe it won't be the greatest thing since Hemingway; therefore, I'd better stop." The result is low frustration tolerance: "It's *too* hard to overcome this difficult passage, and I'm never going to be a marvelous writer as I *should* be—what's the use?" Now, those are two nutty ideas—how would you dispute them?

CLIENT: I'm sure those are both irrational ideas, but one of them is very difficult for me to dispute. If I'm going to be mediocre, why bother? What's the point of being another mediocre writer?

ELLIS: Well, there are a couple of disputes to that. Let's suppose you say, "Well, so far this thing I'm working on is not the Great American Novel—it looks mediocre, and I might as well not finish it." How would you answer that?

CLIENT: I could dispute it by first reminding myself that I don't yet know what my capacity is, or what kind of work I might be able to produce with diligence. Second, I could tell myself that a lot of the value of doing this work is that it's an activity I find worthwhile and a way I'd like to live my life. There's something to be gained in the process of doing it, and it's best not judged on the basis of whether the results bring me some kind of benefit.

Now that the client has cited a particular problem (i.e., difficulties in pursuing the task of writing), Ellis is able to ask an accessing question intended to assist the client in Detecting specific irrational beliefs. It is noted that here he does not merely "tell" the client the nature of these beliefs, but proceeds in a fashion which requires the client to do some introspective thinking. Ellis elaborates upon the response which the client makes, and

MUSEO CASTAGNINO
ROSARIO - ARGENTINA
FUNDACION

Stand de las Artes

MC

he might Debate the beliefs which were identi-
the client initially demurs in the face of this
es him to try to respond. He does, and Ellis

both good disputes. The second one reminds me of
mous statement: "Anything that's worth doing is
ly." A lot of Sunday painters will never produce a
d yet they enjoy the activity. So the writing could be
e challenge of doing it well could be enjoyable, even if
well. Now, once you accept that, you can go back to,
chance it won't be a work of genius, but I'm going to
How will I know without trying?"
k that I'm reaching for my level of incompetence. It's
for me to be something within my capability—I want
ething . . .

ELLIS: But I suspect you're sneaking in a must: "If I reach for a greater level of competence, I must . . . ," what?

CLIENT: I must succeed.

ELLIS: That's right! You see, you're saying, "I have to," instead of, "I'd like to." You *don't* have to.

(For the sake of brevity, a portion of the session has been deleted at this point. This portion consisted largely of a discussion of writers who became successful only after having made several failed attempts at publishing a novel.)

ELLIS: Now, let's take the writing—what minimum amount of writing could you produce per week? In other words, how many pages or hours *minimum* could you devote to it each week?

CLIENT: Well, I'll take time as the unit rather than words or pages. And I would say it should be in ascending increments, just like anything else you might want to get used to. I think two hours each day would be a good starting point.

ELLIS: All right—let's just suppose that for the next week you'll write a minimum of two hours per day. Now, if you wanted to, you could reinforce yourself by doing something easy and enjoyable *after* you finish the two hours. What do you like to do that you normally do every day?

CLIENT: Oh, fiction-reading is a real treat.

ELLIS: So you'll do *no* fiction-reading 'till after the two hours. Also, you could give yourself a penalty if you *don't* do it. What do you hate to do that you normally avoid doing?

CLIENT: Oh . . . housecleaning.

ELLIS: Right—if midnight arrives and you *still* haven't done that two hours, you can stay up for an hour or two doing housecleaning. Now if you really followed that, it wouldn't *make* you do the two hours, but it would definitely encourage you. You reinforce yourself when you

CLIENT: complete the two hours, and penalize yourself when you don't. Let's see what you do when you really try that schedule.

CLIENT: I'll have to give myself a penalty for not imposing the penalty, too!

ELLIS: (Chuckles) Yes, that's true—if you say, "This penalty is *too* hard; I shouldn't have to do it," then in all probability you'll goof off. Getting started is difficult, but once you get into the habit of doing the two hours, it can become routine and easy.

In this passage the client again makes statements which indicate the presence of interfering cognitions, so Ellis quickly asks him to identify his operative "must." This then creates an opportunity to Debate the idea that, "I *must* know that I will succeed before I try to improve," which could assist the client in circumventing another obstacle to the pursuit of his goals.

The session concludes with Ellis helping the client to design a behavioral homework assignment which employs contingency contracting. Such an assignment can be considered more characteristic of somewhat later sessions, as homework assignments stemming from earlier sessions tend to emphasize acquisition of RET's central content material (primarily through bibliotherapy), the identification of irrational beliefs, and cognitive disputation. It is noted that even as the session draws to a close, Ellis continues to emphasize the potential obstacles produced by irrational beliefs.

TEACHING DISPUTATION SKILLS: SUMMARY AND DISCUSSION

In terms of teaching the skills necessary for cognitive modification, Ellis employs differing sets of strategies with clients in earlier and later sessions. The foregoing transcripts can serve to highlight some of these differences:

1. During earlier sessions, Ellis will devote considerable time to teaching the basic tenets of RET. In later sessions, he will make attempts at getting clients to independently utilize these tenets in terms of understanding and overcoming their disturbance.

2. Within the earlier phases of therapy, Ellis will take a more active role in disputing clients' irrational beliefs. He will more frequently offer hypotheses as to the nature of these beliefs, provide disputing questions, and also provide a rational response to the disputing question if the client appears to have great difficulty in doing so. Within the later phases of therapy, he seems more likely to turn over the work of disputing to the client. He provides considerably less assistance and somewhat vaguer prompts, as when he simply asks the client in the later session transcript, "How would you answer that?"

3. It is noted that in later sessions, Ellis may be more likely to introduce auxiliary strategies which the client can utilize to assist in the process of cognitive modification. Such strategies may, for example, include the referenting approach described to the client in the second transcript. In addition, greater emphasis may be placed upon *behavioral* disputing: The technique of pushing oneself to engage in behaviors which run counter to one's irrational beliefs. Such disputing employs the principle of cognitive dissonance (Festinger, 1957), which holds that a state of psychological tension will arise when an individual behaves in a manner discrepant from his or her beliefs. Relief from this tension can be attained by altering these beliefs.

With regard to the issue of employing alternative means for overcoming dysfunctional emotions and behaviors, it should be noted that Ellis does not always teach clients to rely upon philosophical disputation of irrational beliefs. As noted in Chapter 1, this procedure may be too complex or abstract to be of much practical benefit to very young or intellectually-limited clients. As such, Ellis may be more prone to teach certain individuals to make use of rational self-statements. These statements can be viewed as stock phrases which can be used to counter particular identified irrational beliefs. In this sense, they are a means by which clients can talk themselves through stressful situations or distressing emotional episodes. From Ellis's perspective, however, the utility of this approach is limited, as it is less likely to result in the types of deep-seated philosophical change which RET advocates.

To aid clients in the process of acquiring disputation skills, Ellis and his associates have developed a number of pre-printed homework sheets. At the Institute for Rational-Emotive Therapy in New York City, for example, a homework sheet designed by Sichel and Ellis (1984) is routinely made available to clients. This sheet (which is reproduced in Table 4.1) contains a list of thirteen common irrational beliefs, with blank spaces which clients can utilize for writing in disputing questions and effective rational beliefs. It can be particularly useful during the earlier phases of therapy, as it provides a structured format for applying an ABC analysis to disturbed emotions and self-defeating behaviors.

TROUBLESHOOTING

According to RET theory, clients are able to make progress in overcoming their dysfunctional emotions and behaviors when they effectively dispute their irrational beliefs. If it is apparent that a given client has learned the essentials of disputation but is failing to experience positive changes, Ellis will conduct a within-session inquiry in order to determine why this is so.

RET SELF-HELP FORM

Institute for Rational-Emotive Therapy
45 East 65th Street, New York, N.Y. 10021
(212) 535-0822

(A) ACTIVATING EVENTS, thoughts, or feelings that happened just before I felt emotionally disturbed or acted self-defeatingly: _____

_____

(C) CONSEQUENCE or CONDITION—disturbed feeling or self-defeating behavior—that I produced and would like to change: _____

_____

(B) BELIEFS—Irrational BELIEFS (IBs) leading to my CONSEQUENCE (emotional disturbance or self-defeating behavior). Circle all that apply to these ACTIVATING EVENTS (A).	**(D) DISPUTES** for each circled IRRATIONAL BELIEF. Examples: *"Why MUST I do very well?" "Where is it written* that I am a BAD PERSON?" *"Where is the evidence* that I MUST be approved or accepted?"	**(E) EFFECTIVE RATIONAL BELIEFS (RBs)** to replace my IRRATIONAL BELIEFS (IBs). Examples: *"I'd PREFER to do very well but I don't HAVE TO." "I am a PERSON WHO acted badly, not a BAD PERSON." "There is no evidence that I HAVE TO be approved, though I would LIKE to be."*
1. I MUST do well or very well!		
2. I am a BAD OR WORTHLESS PERSON when I act weakly or stupidly.		
3. I MUST be approved or accepted by people I find important!		
4. I NEED to be loved by someone who matters to me a lot!		
5. I am a BAD, UNLOVABLE PERSON if I get rejected.		
6. People MUST treat me fairly and give me what I NEED!		

(OVER)

TABLE 4.1 RET Self-Help Form

7. People MUST live up to my expectations or it is TERRIBLE!		
8. People who act immorally are undeserving, ROTTEN PEOPLE!		
9. I CAN'T STAND really bad things or very difficult people!		
10. My life MUST have few major hassles or troubles.		
11. It's AWFUL or HORRIBLE when major things don't go my way!		
12. I CAN'T STAND IT when life is really unfair!		
13. I NEED a good deal of immediate gratification and HAVE to feel miserable when I don't get it!		
Additional Irrational Beliefs:		

(F) FEELINGS and BEHAVIORS I experienced after arriving at my EFFECTIVE RATIONAL BELIEFS: _____

I WILL WORK HARD TO REPEAT MY EFFECTIVE RATIONAL BELIEFS FORCEFULLY TO MYSELF ON MAN' OCCASIONS SO THAT I CAN MAKE MYSELF LESS DISTURBED NOW AND ACT LESS SELF-DEFEATINGLY IN TH FUTURE.

TABLE 4.1 (continued)

From his perspective, such a situation can indicate that philosophies of low frustration tolerance (LFT) and/or self-rating are in operation (Ellis, 1985a). With regard to the former type of philosophy, a client may subscribe to the irrational belief that "It *must* be easier than it is to adopt a more rational perspective, and I *can't stand* the hard work required to approach this goal." This belief could lead the client to conclude that disputing is "too hard," with the result that efforts towards cognitive modification are weak or non-existent. With regard to the latter philosophy, the client may believe that, "I *should* be making better progress in disputing my irrational beliefs; the fact that I'm not is proof that I am an inadequate, hopeless person." The global negative self-evaluation contained in this sequence of cognitions could lead the individual to erroneously conclude that he/she is incapable of changing, once again resulting in inadequate efforts at disputing.

The brief transcript that follows provides an example of the manner in which Ellis conducts a troubleshooting inquiry. It is drawn from a session with a middle-aged, depressed, alcoholic male client, and focuses upon the obstacles created by his self-rating philosophy:

> ELLIS: Do you do anything to *contradict* your self-downing, or do you just let it go on?
>
> CLIENT: I guess I do virtually nothing.
>
> ELLIS: All right, why is that? Why don't you contradict it?
>
> CLIENT: I guess I believe that I'll never get out of this mess—I'll never really change.
>
> ELLIS: Because . . . ?
>
> CLIENT: Because I'm not strong-willed enough, man enough . . .
>
> ELLIS: But you see, that *is* the self-downing: First, "I'm doing badly," which is a correct perception, and then second, "I'm really a turd who cannot do better." As long as you go along with that, you'll frequently *not* do better! Now, how would you go about disputing that?
>
> CLIENT: (Hesitantly) I'd tell myself that because I've screwed up, and am overdrinking and oversmoking . . . that those are unfortunate and negative actions, but they don't negate my basic worth. Therefore, even though it's unfortunate, it's not the end of the world; it's not a catastrophe because I can still proceed to improve.
>
> That's the only counter-message I can think of, and I'm not terribly convinced of it even as I say it.
>
> ELLIS: *What* is unconvincing? Let's track that down!

At this point, the session continues with Ellis uncovering the client's beliefs that his past patterns of behavior are immutable, and that they must necessarily continue to influence his functioning in the present. As the session concludes, Ellis reinforces the notion that the client has acquired certain useful "insights," but states that the challenge now facing him is to apply these insights in a manner which will assist him in combatting his irrational beliefs: "The problem is to *see* what's going on, to *use* your knowledge, and to *fight* against the nonsense that produces your upsets."

NOTE

1. Referenting (Danysh, 1974) is a technique stemming from general semantics which involves identifying and reviewing the potential advantages and disadvantages of particular courses of action. As an example, a smoker who is trying to quit can list all of the advantages and disadvantages of smoking versus not smoking. By regularly reviewing these lists and focusing upon the advantages of smoking cessation and the disadvantages of continuing this habit, progress towards the goal of nonsmoking might be facilitated.

5

Using Homework Assignments in Therapy

> In RET in particular, we induce individual and group therapy clients to do considerable work in between sessions. . . . We show them how to dispute irrational thinking on many occasions during the week, not merely during therapy sessions. (Ellis & Harper, 1975, p. 6)

Along with such individuals as Salter (1949), Kelly (1955), and Wolpe (1959), Albert Ellis can be regarded as one of the early pioneers in the use of therapeutic homework assignments. Currently, such assignments can be considered an integral component of many approaches to behavior and cognitive-behavior therapy. This view was substantiated by a fairly recent survey of the behavior therapy literature, which indicated that 68% of the outpatient treatment articles published in selected behavior therapy journals between 1973 and 1980 made use of some form of extra-therapy assignment (Shelton & Levy, 1981).

Homework assignments have been an important part of RET since its inception, as their use is consistent with Ellis's concern in practicing effective and efficient psychotherapy. As noted in the introductory chapter, homework assignments serve to extend treatment time and can increase the likelihood that clients will attribute therapeutic change to their own, as opposed to their therapists' efforts. In addition, as noted by other writers, such assignments function to enhance the transfer of learning from the therapy session to the client's natural environment (Levy & Carter, 1976; Shelton & Ackerman, 1974).

Homework assignments serve useful functions *within* therapy sessions as well. Reviewing a prior week's homework, for instance, provides continuity between sessions and establishes an agenda and structure for the current session. Such review can also assist in the process of translating clients' presenting problems from an abstract to a more concrete and immediate level. As an example of this principle, a therapist might give a socially anxious client the homework assignment of attempting to initiate a conversation with an attractive stranger at a party. If an inquiry conducted during the following week's session reveals that the client experienced psychologically-based difficulties in attempting to implement this assignment, session time can be devoted to identification and remediation of the specific obstacles involved. This type of approach can be considered more helpful than interminable intellectual discussions regarding the general topic of "shyness."

The preceding paragraphs have provided an overview of the potential benefits of practicing homework-based psychotherapy. The sections that follow will detail the manner in which Ellis applies this approach within three separate contexts: Public demonstrations of RET, group therapy sessions, and individual therapy sessions. The chapter will conclude with a general critique and discussion of Ellis's utilization of homework assignments.

PUBLIC DEMONSTRATIONS OF RET

Ellis has provided public demonstrations of RET within a wide variety of settings and contexts apart from the Institute for Rational-Emotive Therapy in New York City. At the Institute, however, he gives such demonstrations on a weekly basis at the Friday evening workshop entitled, "Problems of Daily Living." This workshop serves as a vehicle for teaching the general public about the rational-emotive approach to remediation of emotional and behavioral disturbance, while at the same time allowing two volunteers from the audience to separately receive therapeutic assistance with their psychological problems.

In describing the format of these Friday evening workshops, Dryden and Backx (1987) have stated that it is possible to identify a discernible process to the interviews Ellis conducts with his volunteer "clients." The initial portion of this interview is devoted to eliciting a description of a problem of relevance to the client, identifying the client's operative irrational beliefs, and then disputing these irrational beliefs in a forceful and often humorous fashion.[1] Subsequent to these activities, Ellis usually gives the client an *in vivo* lesson in the use of rational-emotive imagery (or REI, described in Chapter 1). Independent practice of this technique is usually suggested for Friday evening workshop volunteers, as Ellis believes that it will assist these individuals in their endeavors to adopt a more rational philosophy.

Within the context of his Friday evening workshops, Ellis tends to be quite consistent with regard to the manner in which he demonstrates and assigns REI as a therapeutic homework activity. The following excerpt, drawn from a public demonstration with a woman with public-speaking anxiety, serves to illustrate his routine for doing so. As the excerpt begins, he is speaking directly to the volunteer:

ELLIS: Now let's give you some rational-emotive imagery, which is a technique created by Maxie Maultsby, Jr. We've already been doing a lot of disputing, but this is a somewhat different way of changing your irrational beliefs—a more dramatic and emotive way.

Close your eyes, and imagine that you're about to give a talk in front of an audience of highly critical people. You're about to give a presentation, and you're pretty sure they're going to pounce on you. They'll say, "Oh, she's a terrible speaker, she doesn't know what she's talking about," et cetera. Can you vividly imagine that happening?

CLIENT: Yes.

ELLIS: Now, how do you feel in your gut as you imagine that occurring? What's your honest feeling?

CLIENT: I'm feeling very anxious.

ELLIS: All right—let yourself feel very anxious. Get in touch with your anxiety and *implode* that feeling. (Pause.) Now that you're feeling very anxious, make yourself feel—instead—merely *concerned* about giving this talk. You can change your anxiety and horror so that you're only feeling appropriately concerned. Tell me when you're feeling only concerned, and not anxious. (Pause.) Did you do it?

CLIENT: Yes, I did.

ELLIS: All right, open your eyes and tell me how you did it. What did you do?

CLIENT: I thought in my mind that even if I do give a lousy presentation and get criticized, it's not the end of the world. And I reminded myself that it's unlikely that everyone in the audience would be critical of me.

ELLIS: Right—that was very good! You showed yourself that you could *survive* a lousy presentation, and also saw that different people in the audience will probably experience different kinds of feelings towards you and your talk.

Now, what I want you to do is practice this rational-emotive imagery every day for the next thirty days. One, make yourself anxious by imagining the worst possible thing, and two, *change* that feeling to one of mere concern. You can do that in the ways you just described, as well as in other ways that will occur to you. Do it every day until you get very practiced at it and automatically tend to feel that more appropriate way. Will you continue to do that once a day for the next thirty days?

CLIENT: If it will help get over my anxiety, I definitely will.

ELLIS: Just in case you don't—although I think you probably will—we'll give you a reinforcement and a penalty. That will help you to make sure you do it. First, what do you like to do that you do almost every day of the week?

CLIENT: Oh—I like jogging.

ELLIS: Okay, for the next thirty days no jogging until *after* you do the rational-emotive imagery. You can get up at six o'clock in the morning and do the rational-emotive imagery—and it only took you about a minute and a half to do it just now—and *then* go jogging. What do you *hate* to do that you normally avoid doing?

CLIENT: Cleaning the bathroom.

ELLIS: Right. For the next thirty days, if midnight comes and you still haven't done the rational-emotive imagery, you're going to clean that god-damned bathroom until it shines! If you *do* the rational-emotive imagery you can boycott the bathroom for the whole month!

Now, is there anything about your problem that we haven't covered yet? Did we miss any important aspect of it?

CLIENT: No, I think we really covered it!

ELLIS: (Referring to the audience at the workshop.) All right, let's get *their* comments. We'll pass around the microphone . . .

(At this point of the demonstration, members of the workshop are provided with the opportunity to ask questions or offer advice relevant to the volunteer's problem.)

As can be seen in this excerpt, the manner in which Ellis assigns independent practice of REI to workshop volunteers is likely to increase the probability of homework compliance. He is quite specific as to the homework activity which is to be enacted, as he first takes the volunteer through an REI induction and then later reiterates the technique's essential components ("One, make yourself anxious . . . and two, *change* that feeling to one of mere concern"). He also provides a rationale for implementing this assignment (". . . this is a somewhat different way of changing your irrational beliefs—a more dramatic and emotive way"), and is specific as to the frequency and duration of implementation (". . . every day for the next thirty days"). Finally, he works with the client to identify meaningful consequences for both compliance and non-compliance. As Dryden and Backx (1987) point out, this "operant conditioning" (as Ellis refers to it) is intended to provide the client with a source of motivation for carrying out the homework task.[2]

While Ellis regularly utilizes several compliance-enhancement procedures at his Friday evening workshops, it is noted that these demonstrations represent one-time therapeutic contacts for many volunteers. As such, it is difficult to determine whether these procedures are having the desired effect, and whether clients are benefitting from their use of REI. Research on this issue could prove worthwhile and interesting, as it would represent an assessment of the therapeutic worth of such public demonstrations.

GROUP THERAPY SESSIONS

At the Institute for Rational-Emotive Therapy in New York City, Ellis typically leads five group therapy sessions per week. His groups usually contain between 7 and 10 clients,[3] and last approximately two and a quarter hours. Ellis leads the first hour and a half of the group in his office with the assistance of one or more co-therapists; following this period, the group moves from Ellis's office to another nearby room where the co-therapists act as leaders for the remaining session time.[4]

During a group therapy session, each client receives approximately 15 to 20 minutes to discuss a personal problem. Clients usually receive a homework assignment at the end of their "turns." These homework assignments are generally tailored to the individual client and the problem currently under consideration, and may be suggested by Ellis, a co-therapist, or other members of the group.[5] It is intended, of course, that each client will make some attempt to implement their homework activity between group sessions.

All homework assignments are recorded in writing by the co-therapists, such that group session notes can later be forwarded to Ellis. Table 5.1 provides a facsimile of group session notes, and serves to illustrate the types of activities that may be assigned. As can be seen, these homeworks are largely behavioral and cognitive in nature, and are tailored to each individual client within the group.

During the following week's group session, Ellis generally begins each client's turn with review of the prior week's homework. If a client's report concerning the homework is indicative of non-compliance or difficulties with implementation, some time may be devoted to troubleshooting. Typically, such troubleshooting is focused upon identifying and disputing interfering irrational beliefs. The troublesome homework may then be reassigned in its original form, or somehow modified to increase the probability of successful enactment.

Because of the presence of other clients, Ellis's therapy groups can represent an especially powerful vehicle for dealing with the problem of homework non-compliance. Group members will often offer each other mutual support and encouragement when obstacles to homework completion are encountered, and will occasionally be quite confrontative when it is perceived that a given individual is simply "copping out." In addition, group members who usually work at their homework assignments serve as important models for those who tend to be non-compliant, as they will generally progress more quickly in therapy.

In concluding this section, it is noted that Ellis will periodically encourage all members of each therapy group to undertake shame-attacking exercises (or shame attacks). As noted in Chapter 1, these exercises require

Wednesday Night Group - 7:30 p.m.
Co-leaders: Mike & Nancy
Group Members: Bill, Diana, Rhonda, Christopher, Debbie, Mitch
Absent Member: Lisa

<u>Homework Assignments</u>:
<u>Debbie</u>: Use REI to help yourself to be merely concerned (rather than anxious) with regard to your upcoming presentation at work.

<u>Bill</u>: Practice saying "no" to unreasonable requests by family members and co-workers. Remind yourself that you don't <u>need</u> their approval!

<u>Rhonda</u>: Work at completing your resume, as per the schedule discussed in group. Use rewards & penalties to help yourself do it.

<u>Diana</u>: Stick to your plan to cut down to 5 cigarettes per day. Fight your LFT by disputing the belief that, "I <u>must</u> smoke when I have the urge!"

<u>Christopher</u>: Work on your anger at your wife by challenging your belief that, "She <u>must</u> treat me with consideration at all times."

<u>Mitch</u>: When out on date this weekend, practice conversational skills. Work on overcoming the demand that, "I <u>must</u> say interesting and witty things."

TABLE 5.1 Facsimile of Group Session Notes

clients to engage purposely in (non-harmful) behaviors that are likely to be regarded by observers as silly or foolish. Clients who complete shame attacks can learn that they are able to withstand the discomfort associated with the disapproval of others, and that they don't have to engage in self-downing when they behave in less than exemplary ways. When group members collectively report on their shame attack experiences during the following week's group session, they are able to compare notes and to perhaps see even more strongly (as a result of group consensus) that the consequences of foolish behavior are not horrible. Reluctant clients in particular may stand to benefit from the reports of their fellows, as this "proves" that even they can survive this exercise.

INDIVIDUAL THERAPY SESSIONS

In the earlier sessions of this therapy, Ellis appears to employ a somewhat standard set of homework assignments. At the conclusion of a brand new client's first session, for instance, he can almost always be heard giving the directive to "read the pamphlets" and one or two of his self-help books.[6] Such an assignment is relatively easy for most clients to do, so it stands a good chance of completion. As such, it may set the stage for compliance with later homework assignments. In addition, clients who complete this assignment provide themselves with a grounding in rational-emotive theory and techniques, which can serve to save them treatment time. If the client acquires some basic knowledge of the ABC model and the role of irrational beliefs in producing emotional upsets, then time may not have to be devoted to presenting this material during actual therapy sessions.

Instructions to monitor one's upsets during the week represent another type of homework assignment that is often presented to clients during the earlier sessions of therapy. Thus, Ellis might give the following directive to a given client: "When you really get upset about anything, write it down and bring it in next time. I'll show you your must, and what to do about it." This type of homework is intended to facilitate the task of showing clients how their upsets stem from their particular set of irrational beliefs. The ABC model is applied to the upsets that the client brings in to the session, and hypotheses are advanced regarding the musts and shoulds to which the client subscribes. This homework assignment may also be especially useful with clients who tend to be unfocused and rambling during therapy sessions, as it can serve to focus session time on one or two specific emotional problems.

As a slightly more advanced variation on the above theme, Ellis may instruct clients to monitor their *thoughts* when they are upset: "Next time you're angry, look at your thinking—look for the must!" This homework, of course, presupposes that the client has some willingness to consider the notion that thoughts create feelings. If clients engage in thought-monitoring but are unable to accurately identify their irrational beliefs, Ellis will spend session time showing them the demands that lie behind the thoughts of which they *are* aware. He then teaches them how to dispute these demands.

Even during his very first session with a given client, Ellis will make statements concerning the therapeutic importance of effecting profound philosophical modifications. As therapy proceeds beyond the early stages, he tends to increase his emphasis upon inter-session practice of skills related to disputation and the use of rational self-statements. Ellis's directives concerning such homework activities are usually delivered at several points within his sessions, as opposed to being presented only as the sessions draw to a close. As a result, he has ample opportunity to provide clarification and instruction when clients express confusion as to the "when and how" of homework implementation.

Ellis is also more likely to emphasize activity-oriented homework assignments as therapy continues. Many such assignments incorporate a "flooding" approach, wherein the client pursues full *in vivo* exposure to distress-provoking stimuli while resisting the usual urges towards avoidance or escape. Thus, a non-assertive female client may be advised to request a long overdue raise from her boss, while the male client who makes himself angry at his mother-in-law might be instructed to telephone her (and attempt to feel and act non-angrily) several times during the week. Ellis favors the flooding approach to activity-oriented assignments, as it can provide clients with good opportunities to practice their disputing skills. Exposure to the situations most strongly associated with emotional and behavioral upsets may serve to trigger clients' "hot cognitions" (meaning irrational beliefs in the present context), thus allowing these individuals to become more adept at identifying and altering their maladaptive thinking styles. Also, high-level exposure of this type can help clients to see that they are able to withstand unpleasant circumstances and emotional discomfort.

As with homework assignments aimed primarily at cognitive modification, suggestions concerning activity-oriented assignments are often sprinkled throughout Ellis's sessions. It is important to note, however, that Ellis appears to employ the latter type of assignment with less frequency.

CRITIQUE AND DISCUSSION

In reviewing Ellis's utilization of homework assignments within therapy sessions and public demonstrations, it seems possible to identify a number of points where he is vulnerable to criticism. The present section will outline these potential areas of weakness, and will attempt to address each one.

First, it is noted that many individuals who practice homework-based psychotherapy would emphasize the importance of "negotiating" homework assignments with clients. In this context, negotiation refers to a process wherein therapist and client work together to design homework assignments. This collaborative approach is usually viewed by such therapists as a means for enhancing homework compliance, as it is deemed likely to result in assignments which the client is willing to undertake and sees as relevant to his or her problems. Ellis, however, seems to largely eschew this collaborative approach in favor of a more authoritative stance. Hence, he will most often simply make direct suggestions and recommendations regarding the homework activities which he sees as most beneficial. From his perspective, an overly collaborative approach can compromise the therapy, as it has the potential to produce homework assignments which are both less efficient and less effective. By negotiating, the overly collaborative therapist runs the risk of placing a tacit stamp of approval upon therapeutically-weaker homework activities.

Second, review of Ellis's audiotaped sessions suggests that he doesn't typically begin his individual (as opposed to group) therapy contacts by reviewing the client's implementation of previously-assigned homework. This is another point for potential criticism, as such review (as noted earlier in this chapter) can serve to provide continuity between sessions and establish an agenda for the current session. Ellis, however, has stated that he prefers to allow clients to set the goals for each of their sessions with him (Warren, McLellarn, & Ellis, 1987). In this way, he avoids focusing the session's content upon issues which might be of relatively little interest to the client. It is noted, however, that if clients spontaneously bring up difficulties with homework implementation as a concern they wish to address, Ellis will devote session time to remediation of these problems. Ellis is not directive in the sense of establishing specific goals for each of his sessions; rather, he is directive in terms of having overall or general goals (such as self-acceptance and long-range hedonism) which he believes are beneficial for clients to approach. Within group therapy sessions, on the other hand, Ellis is usually quite consistent in reviewing the prior week's homework assignment with each group member. This is because group members generally have less time to discuss problems than do clients in individual therapy; as such, it is desirable to impose some extra structure upon the manner in which the group session proceeds.

Third, it is possible to accuse Ellis of not devoting sufficient time to the assignment of homework activities within his therapy sessions. In this vein, Becker and Rosenfeld (1976) reported that while Ellis gave homeworks in 75% of the audiotaped initial sessions they reviewed, the actual assignment of homework frequently consisted of just one statement and so constituted a relatively small percentage of his overall comments. This observation can seemingly lend itself to a significant criticism, as clients may be uncertain and confused regarding homework assignments if they are not provided with sufficient details concerning means for implementation. In addressing this point, however, it is first noted that the study cited above examined twenty tape recordings of Ellis's *initial* individual therapy sessions. These first sessions usually include a bibliotherapy assignment (". . . read the pamphlets . . ."); such an assignment does not require elaborate explanations regarding enactment. Next, it is noted that Ellis tends to emphasize homework assignments aimed at cognitive modification during his individual therapy sessions. While it might be argued that his directives concerning such assignments are too brief and lack sufficient detail, it has to be acknowledged that the vast majority of his sessions are focused mainly upon teaching and demonstrating disputation skills. In a sense then, almost all of Ellis's sessions can be viewed as preparing the client for independent application of these skills.

Finally, Ellis has been criticized for overemphasizing cognitive homework assignments at the expense of assignments which tend to be more activity-oriented. This observation, in fact, was made by Lazarus (1989) in a recent review of Ellis's practice of RET. While the audiotape review which formed the basis for the current book does indeed suggest that Ellis employs cognitively-oriented homework with greater frequency than activity-oriented homework, it is important to recognize that the apparent emphasis on the former type of assignment is consistent with Ellis's views on the practice of effective therapy. In short, Ellis (1988) contends that therapies that promote profound philosophic modifications are likely to help clients attain positive and lasting changes in their feelings and behavior. This is because, in his view, cognition, emotion, and behavior overlap and influence each other to a significant degree. As such, he states that ". . . profound philosophic changes are likely to be comprised of fairly hot cognitions that include *strong* feeling and action tendencies" (Ellis, 1988, p. 398). It seems clear that Ellis regards cognitive modification as quite often representing the best route to successful treatment.

In conclusion, most aspects of Ellis's approach to utilizing homework assignments can be considered consistent with his own philosophy and practice propositions concerning the conduct of effective therapy. Obviously, however, it is not incumbent upon the reader to accept Ellis's views (and practices) in this regard. Just as Ellis's positions on psychotherapy are based upon his own clinical experiences and researches, it is preferable for each individual practitioner to conduct a careful assessment of the information at his or her disposal prior to accepting a particular therapeutic approach as valid.

NOTES

1. It is important to note that the humor employed by Ellis is directed at ridiculing the client's irrational beliefs, not the client him or herself. Ellis's use of humor receives detailed treatment in Chapter 10, "The Use of Humor in Psychotherapy."

2. The reader will recall that Ellis made use of this procedure with a client during a regular therapy session in the second audiotape transcript presented in Chapter 4 (see pp. 57–58).

3. In the past, Ellis's therapy groups could contain as many as thirteen clients. Limiting groups to ten participants represents a relatively recent change that he has implemented.

4. The co-therapists in Ellis's groups are generally either psychology interns or mental health professionals enrolled in the Institute's Fellowship training program.

5. Ellis and the co-therapists monitor the homework assignments suggested by other group members. If such an assignment appears ineffective or potentially harmful, they will advise against its implementation and suggest a more therapeutic alternative.

6. New clients at the Institute for Rational-Emotive Therapy receive a free packet of pamphlets and reprints dealing with various aspects of RET when they come for their first appointment.

In a recent article reviewing Ellis's responses to a survey of rational-emotive therapists (Warren, McLellarn, & Ellis, 1987), Ellis reported that he uses bibliotherapy with 100% of his clients. He further stated that the self-help books he most frequently suggests are:

   a. *A New Guide to Rational Living* (Ellis & Harper, 1975)—Suggested to 90% of clients.
   b. *A Guide to Personal Happiness* (Ellis & Becker, 1982)—Suggested to 95% of clients.
   c. *Overcoming Procrastination* (Ellis & Knaus, 1977)—Suggested to 40% of clients.

Although not indicated in his responses to the survey, Ellis (personal communication, September 1989) has noted that he now suggests his recently published book, *How to Stubbornly Refuse to Make Yourself Miserable About Anything—Yes, Anything*, to over 95% of his clients.

6

Imparting a Rational Philosophy of Life

The essential basis for improvement or change in the individual in the course of RT[1] is considered to be not the removal of presenting symptoms but a significant, deepseated, and lasting change in his or her basic philosophy of life; especially in the view that anxiety and hostility are necessary correlates of living. (Ellis, 1963, p. 5)

As the above quote indicates, the emphasis of Ellis's approach to therapy is not upon mere symptom removal. Rather than simply assisting his psychotherapy clients to *feel* better, Ellis attempts to help them *get* better by facilitating profound modifications in the manner in which they view themselves, other people, and the world around them (Ellis, 1972a). For reasons that will be discussed, he believes that this particular focus in psychotherapy is likely to result in more significant and lasting benefits to clients than therapies—such as certain forms of behavior and strategic therapy—which stress only the alleviation of clients' presenting symptoms. In his view, such therapies are ultimately less helpful—and perhaps even somewhat harmful— to clients.

According to Ellis (1980b), quick removal of presenting symptoms may actually discourage clients from working to root out the true underlying causes of their emotional and behavioral problems. Thus, they may miss the opportunity to learn the means for identifying and altering self-defeating belief systems. Ellis hypothesizes that as a result of this omission, the possibility that other disturbing symptoms might later spring up is greatly increased. These potential future difficulties are not viewed as representing symptom-substitution in the classic psychoanalytic sense, but are seen as derivatives of the irrational beliefs with which the client originally entered therapy.

In addition to the possibility of new or recurring symptoms, Ellis (1980b) sees another drawback to symptom-removal approaches to psychotherapy: Clients who experience swift amelioration of their distress may conclude that there are easy (and lasting) solutions to life's difficult problems, and that they absolutely cannot (or shouldn't have to) tolerate any degree of emotional discomfort. Thus, the personal philosophy which leads to low frustration tolerance is reinforced, and the client becomes more vulnerable to the inevitable vicissitudes and hassles of life.

Even in his earliest writings on RET, Ellis (1962, 1963) emphasized the ideological or philosophical basis of emotional disturbance. Since he views the etiological roots of such disturbance as being philosophical in nature, he naturally sets himself the task of assisting clients in the process of attaining a broad reorientation of their basic outlooks on life. He believes that when individuals are able to approach the deepseated philosophical changes which he advocates, it is possible for them to reach the following goals:

1. Removal of their original presenting symptoms.
2. The ability to cope with and eliminate any new symptoms which might arise, and
3. The potential to avoid or ward off the development of new symptoms.

From Ellis's perspective, the process of helping clients to make broad changes in their personal philosophies consists of a great deal more than just showing them how their main irrational beliefs are contributing to their current emotional and behavioral problems. In his view, it is also important that they come away from therapy with some knowledge of other common irrational beliefs to which human beings typically subscribe—thus armed, they may be less likely to fall prey to other dysfunctional belief systems in the future. In addition, it is considered important not only to eradicate clients' irrational patterns of thinking, emoting, and acting, but to provide them with an understanding of the tenets of a more rational philosophy of life.

RET is a form of psychotherapy which attempts to help individuals prolong their lives, experience a minimum of emotional disturbance, and actualize themselves. In prior writings, Ellis (1967, 1987a; Ellis & Bernard, 1985) set forth what are described as the main values or goals of RET. These goals, which include the following, can be considered as the components of a rational philosophy of life:

1. *Self-interest*: While emotionally healthy people will occasionally and selectively subordinate their own wants and preferences to those of others,

they mainly tend to give at least slightly more importance to their own interests.

2. *Social interest*: Emotionally mature individuals are interested in the welfare of others, engage in behaviors that will benefit the social group, and strive to cultivate pleasurable interpersonal relationships.

3. *Self direction*: Emotionally healthy people assume responsibility for themselves, and are not dependent upon support or approval from others.

4. *Tolerance*: Healthy individuals separate the rating of a person from the rating of his or her behaviors. Even though they may dislike it when others act poorly, they refrain from condemning and negatively rating these others in their totality.

5. *Acceptance of uncertainty*: Emotionally healthy people recognize that there are no guarantees in life. They are able to approach life in a probabilistic manner and do not demand to know what the future holds in store.

6. *Flexibility/Scientific thinking*: Healthy individuals are non-rigid in their thinking, and can revise their hypotheses about the world when confronted with convincing evidence.

7. *Commitment*: Emotionally healthy people frequently have some creative interest or pursuit which they find vitally absorbing. While they would tend not to sacredize this interest, they may structure a good part of their lives around it.

8. *Risk-taking*: People who are emotionally healthy are more open to taking reasonable risks in order to achieve the goals they set for themselves. They tend not to awfulize about the possibility of failure.

9. *Self-acceptance*: Healthy individuals accept the fact that they have both good and bad characteristics and behaviors. They tend not to rate their worth as persons on the basis of their performance or the amount of approval they receive from others.

10. *Long-range hedonism*: Emotionally well-adjusted people are generally not short-sighted, and act in ways which will maximize their pleasure and sense of fulfillment in life. They tend to be willing to endure present pain for long-range gain.

11. *Nonutopianism*: Healthy people accept the fact that both they and the world are imperfect, and that it is impossible to have only pleasure and avoid all pain. Nevertheless, they determine to make the best of conditions as they exist.

12. *Self-responsibility for own emotional disturbance*: Emotionally mature individuals understand and accept the fact that they create their emotional upsets, rather than blaming these disturbances on conditions or other people.

Teaching these goals or values to clients represents a rather monumental task, especially when one considers the fact that RET is intended to be a relatively brief form of psychotherapy. Ensuring that clients will acquire and apply the tenets of a rational philosophy of life requires patience, repetition, and a large degree of flexibility and creativity on the part of the therapist.

Ellis is most often quite explicit and direct in his communications to clients during psychotherapy sessions, and his reputation in the field is based partly upon these qualities. Review of his audiotaped sessions, however, reveals that he also employs less direct modes of communication, including metaphors and stories. In addition, he makes frequent use of self-disclosure during psychotherapy, and invents unusual, humorous slogans which clients can remember long after their sessions are over. It can be hypothesized that by using these various "media," Ellis increases his effectiveness as a teacher of the principles of sound mental health. The sections that follow will present an overview of Ellis's use of these various methods of communication as a means for imparting a rational philosophy of life. Excerpts from his audiotapes will be presented in order to illustrate each type.

DIRECT TEACHING

In RET, the process of disputing irrational beliefs results in clients achieving a more realistic and adaptive way of viewing themselves and their conditions. While Ellis will often begin showing clients disputation strategies by actively questioning and refuting their demands, musts, and shoulds within sessions, he also teaches these strategies through direct description. As noted in Chapter 4, he generally describes the use of disputing questions in easily understandable terms, as illustrated by the following brief exchange:

> CLIENT: I guess I'm telling myself that I *must* have their approval.
> ELLIS: That's right! Now, how would you dispute that?
> CLIENT: I'm not sure . . .
> ELLIS: The dispute is merely, "Why?" First you find the must—then all you have to do is put a "why" in front of it and forcefully ask yourself, "Why the fuck *must* I have their approval?"

In addition to directly teaching clients techniques for disputing their irrational beliefs, Ellis teaches them the importance of continued and consistent disputation. Thus, he can often be heard making statements such as these:

> "If you'll show yourself many times that you don't *need* what you want, then you'll solve the problem."

"Go over it and over it until you convince yourself: People *are* the way they are! Tough shit!"

"Can you see the important thing? Your demands will return to smite you, unless you keep working at giving them up!"

"The problem is to *use* the tools [i.e., disputing techniques]. Unless you actively contradict your absolute shoulds, they'll probably plague you forever."

Just as he teaches how and why to dispute, Ellis will also directly describe more rational, effective strategies by which clients can achieve their important life goals. Conceivably, clients could be left totally to their own devices in terms of determining the best route to a given objective, but from the RET perspective this could result in a needless waste of an individual's time and effort. As such, Ellis takes the position that it is better to judiciously offer advice and suggestions. In the following excerpt, he describes a means for finding a suitable male partner to a young female client with a history of unsatisfactory romantic relationships:

The main thing is that you don't seem to go with the right men from the beginning. Although they might be o.k., they don't really suit you—then you stay too long in the relationship and finally leave without an apparent reason. How are you going to get what you really want except by going out, meeting people, eliminating them fast if they're not your cup of tea, and then finally ending up with a good one? If you go through many, you'll find a few.

Suppose you had no job—wouldn't you go about finding a job in the same way? Dating can be a pain in the ass—but unless you figure out a better way, that's how you'll get what you want. If you want the mating, then you go through the goddamn dating!

By making reference to the list of rational-emotive goals and values described earlier, it is possible to see that the advice conveyed in this passage embodies self-direction, acceptance of uncertainty, risk-taking, and long-range hedonism.

MODELING AND SELF-DISCLOSURE

Ellis (1967, 1985a) has indicated that during the process of therapy, the rational-emotive therapist can serve as an important model of a saner, more sensible philosophy of life. In particular, he has stressed the modeling of unconditional acceptance of persons. Thus, he has written that:

If they [clients] become angry at me, as they frequently do, I do *not* return their feelings with anger of my own; and if they indicate that they do not love or approve of me, I do *not* indicate that it is awful, and that I cannot live successfully without their approval. (Ellis, 1967, p. 214)

By having repeated contacts with a therapist who refuses to condemn or blame them even when they behave in an execrable fashion, clients can indirectly learn to accept themselves with their fallibilities and imperfections.

It should be noted, however, that Ellis (1982) believes that an *overemphasis* upon modeling effects can be disadvantageous for clients and the therapy. If, for example, therapists model tolerance, self-direction, and commitment without also actively teaching the means for approaching these goals, particular clients might be prone to engage in a comparison process which ultimately leads them to negative self-rating. In a similar vein, Ellis notes that pure modeling of skills—like that which often occurs in assertion training—is likely to be inefficient because it fails to show clients how to alter the basic irrational beliefs which underlie their self-defeating behavior.

In addition to the effects achieved through rational responses to client behavior within sessions, Ellis selectively employs self-disclosure as yet another vehicle for imparting his philosophical perspective. Although he rarely cites this method in his writings, it is interesting to note that he makes fairly frequent use of it. As such, he can be heard citing various aspects of his background or personal life in approximately 25% of the audiotaped sessions reviewed for this volume.

Generally, it appears that Ellis employs two main types of self-disclosure. First, he will sometimes make reference to personal problems he was able to overcome as a youth (such as shyness and public-speaking anxiety) in order to illustrate strategies for resolving particular types of difficulties. In so doing, he encourages clients that they can accomplish similar objectives if they are willing to undertake the effort involved. Second, he will describe features of his *current* behavior which illustrate how it is guided by a flexible, non-musturbatory philosophy.

The excerpts that follow will serve as examples of both of these forms of self-disclosure. The first, drawn from a session with a 32-year-old socially anxious male, demonstrates self-disclosure in which Ellis makes reference to his own past emotional and behavioral problems. More specifically, he relates the manner in which he managed to overcome his public-speaking anxiety:

The way you conquer social inhibition is by *forcing* yourself to be uncomfortable until you become comfortable. Many years ago when I was just 19, I was scared shitless of public-speaking—I never did it at all! In grade school and high school I always avoided it or got out of it. But then I *forced* myself to do it, knowing that nothing would happen if I fell on my face and they laughed at me. I convinced myself of this and made myself do it uncomfortably, and after about ten times I not only got over my fear of public-speaking—which was really a phobia at the time—but I started to enjoy it and got very good at it. Now, you can't keep me away from the public-speaking platform!

This next excerpt is taken from a session with a 27-year-old man experiencing difficulty in controlling his compulsive eating habits. Here, Ellis describes how he regulates his own eating behavior through rational thinking. The first speaker is the client:

CLIENT: Just this morning I sat down to an enormous breakfast and I asked myself, "Why am I eating all of this?"

ELLIS: Well, what *is* the answer to that question?

CLIENT: My answer was, "I'm hungry"—and I know that isn't the right answer.

ELLIS: That's right—that's not the *full* answer. If I sat down and was as hungry as you, I would only have eaten a little food, like I did this morning. Even though I could eat a big breakfast every morning, I never do—I'm diabetic, you see. I start with the same statement as you: "I'm hungry." But then, I still eat my very small breakfast. Now what makes me eat my very small breakfast even when I'm hungry?

CLIENT: You choose?

ELLIS: That's right! I'd *like* more food because I'm hungry, but the food doesn't like *me* and I don't *have* to have what I'd like! Fuck it! I can't recall that in 25 years I've had a single large breakfast. I just have a piece of bread and two dried pears and take my insulin, and that's my breakfast! Even when I'm travelling on a plane and they serve a big breakfast, I only eat a small portion of it. I wrap up the rest and take it with me!

CLIENT: (Laughs)

ELLIS: They'll give me some ham and bread, and I'll make a sandwich for later. But I don't eat it for breakfast because I'm saying to myself, "I'd *like* this ham sandwich right now but I don't *need* it and I'd better not have it because it will harm me!" Now, you're not saying that—you're saying, "Because I'm hungry I *must* have a hearty breakfast." See the difference? Give up that must and you'll be able to eat a moderate breakfast! (Later in the session:)

CLIENT: When you related that thing about the ham sandwich, I thought, "Isn't that great! He doesn't give a fuck what anybody says about him!" If it were me, I'd worry about what the people around me were thinking as I was wrapping up the food. But you're able to do what's good for you because you don't need their approval!

ELLIS: What's more, if I'm on a public-speaking platform and my time comes for eating—because I eat twelve times a day to balance my insulin—I take out my sandwich and start eating it! People stare—but I'm not ashamed—because what *must* am I *not* saying to myself?

CLIENT: You're saying, "I don't need their approval."

ELLIS: That's right! If they think I'm a nut, they think I'm a nut! There's no reason why they *must* not think I'm crazy or peculiar—if they do, they do.

CLIENT: This story has really hit me—that's a good philosophy of life! I'm always so worried about what everyone else thinks—I'd be much better off if I just focused on what's best for *me*!

ELLIS: Yes! I might not *like* the stewardess or other people to think I'm crazy, but I like *me*, and I'm determined to take care of myself. I'm not going to eat by their schedule because I need their love—I could kill myself that way!

METAPHORS, STORIES, AND SLOGANS

Ellis utilizes therapeutic metaphors, stories and slogans as yet another means for explicating the tenets of a rational philosophy of life. Since he sees his main role as that of teacher, he will make use of virtually any pedagogical device in order to facilitate the client's learning process. Metaphorical devices—which generally represent a more indirect form of communication within psychotherapy—have the potential to leave a lasting impression on clients because they represent a novel deviation from the direct, confrontative approach typically employed by rational-emotive therapists. Unlike therapists from certain other schools, however, Ellis does not overly rely upon such devices in order to *make* his points. Rather, he will use these methods merely to *illustrate* the points he wishes to make. As such, he will usually describe the purpose of a metaphor to a client just prior to delivering it, or will offer a succinct explanation of a story immediately after its telling. The intent of each device is thereby made explicit, and the possibility of misinterpretation is thus reduced.

The following exchange contains a therapeutic metaphor frequently used by Ellis in order to illustrate the rational-emotive conceptualization of emotional disturbance:

ELLIS: Now, let me give you a model that explains the origin of almost *all* neurotic disturbance: Imagine that you go out from here 20 minutes from now, and you don't know how much money you have in your pocket—it could be one dollar, or it could be a thousand—you just don't know. You say to yourself, "I want to have at least ten dollars, just in case I want to go to a movie or get something to eat. I wish, I'd prefer, I'd like to have a minimum of ten dollars." Then, you look in your pocket and find that you have *nine*. Now, how would you feel if that were so?

CLIENT: Disappointed.

ELLIS: That's right! Now imagine that the next time you go out, you're saying to yourself, "I've *got* to have at least ten dollars at all times! I *must*! I absolutely have to have a minimum of ten!" If you really believed that and suddenly found that you had only nine dollars, then how would you feel?

CLIENT: Worse—maybe anxious.

ELLIS: Right! But it isn't the money, you see, that would make you feel upset. It's the *must*. When you elevate your *preference* into a *must*, you make yourself disturbed!

Now finally, you're going out for a third time, and you're still saying the same thing to yourself: "I *must* have a minimum of ten dollars at all times, I need a *guarantee* of ten!" Again you look in your pocket, but this time you have *eleven*! *Now* how would you feel?

CLIENT: Happy!

ELLIS: Right again! *But*, with the eleven still in your pocket, something would occur to you in the next moment that would throw you into a panic. Do you know what that would be?

CLIENT: I might think to myself, "What if I lose it?"

ELLIS: Yes, that's exactly right! You see, your premise is that "I *must* have a minimum of ten at all times. I *now* have eleven, but suppose I [said with prolonged emphasis] L-O-S-E two, suppose I spend two, suppose I get robbed?" Because all of these things could happen.

Now, the point of this model is that whenever any human takes any desire or preference and escalates it into a must, a necessity—they'll be anxious when they don't have what they think they must, and miserable even when they do!

In this excerpt, Ellis provides the client with information about the intent of the metaphor both before and after it is delivered. He presents it as a model of the manner in which human beings create their own emotional disturbance, and reiterates its most important points at its conclusion. Interestingly, this exchange can be considered an "interactive metaphor," as it requires the client's cooperation and participation in order to be successful. This feature increases its value as a therapeutic tool, as it provides Ellis with an opportunity to check the client's understanding and probably increases the likelihood that the content will be remembered. This is because the client is placed in the position of being an active, as opposed to a passive, learner.

Ellis's use of stories during therapy sessions is often directed at illustrating the manner in which absolutistic thinking impacts upon various aspects of cognition, affect, and behavior. Ellis uses the tale that follows to demonstrate the relationship between "musturbation" and obsessive thinking. Here, it is delivered to a young female client troubled by what she describes as lustful thoughts:

The more you say, "I must not think of it, I must not think of it, I must not think of it," the more you'll think of it! As soon as you stick in the must, you become obsessed.

Let me tell you a fable about the king who didn't want to marry off his daughter. She was being courted by a prince, and the prince was very eligible. So the king said to his advisors, "Find me something this son-of-a-bitch can't do! We'll make it a test, and when he fails the test we'll tell him the wedding's off!"

But the king's advisors were unable to find a task the prince couldn't do—he passed every test!

Finally, the king said, "Unless you come up with something soon, I'm going to cut your balls off. I don't want this guy to marry my daughter!"

So, they found something the prince couldn't do—they told him, "Don't think of a pink elephant for 20 minutes." He failed that test as soon as he said to himself, "I must not think of a pink elephant, I must not think of a pink elephant, I must not think of a pink elephant"—for then, of course, he thought of one.

As soon as *you* say, "I must not lust, I must not lust, I must not lust"—I guarantee you'll be obsessed about lusting. That's the way the human mind works! If you said, "I don't want to lust but fuck it—if I do, I do"—then your obsessive thoughts would go away.

During his psychotherapy sessions Ellis will also occasionally tell a "story" about some other client he has seen. Typically, he will give a general description of that individual's presenting problem and the way it is caused and maintained by irrational thinking, and relate this information to the current client's symptoms. Following this, he may describe improvements that this other client has made, emphasizing that such progress was due to the individual's vigorous and consistent efforts at implementing change. Obviously, such clinical tales omit any information that would jeopardize the client's right to confidentiality.

Ellis has an incisive wit and a keen sense of humor, and is well known for his ability to invent slogans which capture the essence of his approach to therapy and life. These slogans are easy to recall and powerful in their impact, as they generally contain an element of surprise or novelty. In this vein, they may employ obscene language, utilize idiosyncratic words, or embody an idea which deviates sharply from the client's usual manner of thinking about things. The following list represents a sample of slogans used by Ellis during therapy sessions. A brief "translation" accompanies each one:

1. *Shouldhood leads to shithood.* This slogan conveys the notion that when human beings apply absolutistic, perfectionistic demands to their own

or others behavior, they increase their likelihood of engaging in negative self or other-rating.

2. *All neurosis is simply a high class name for whining.* Chronic whining results from a philosophy of low frustration tolerance, which is frequently at the core of many clients' presenting complaints.

3. *Masturbation is good and delicious, but musturbation is bad and pernicious.* This slogan can be used to introduce the term "musturbation" into clients' vocabularies. Musturbation refers to the process of engaging in absolutistic, dogmatic thinking, which results in emotional and behavioral upsets.

4. *RET is simple, but it's not easy.* RET's concepts are easier to understand than they are to apply, because application requires more concerted effort. Only through such effort, however, is an individual likely to overcome his or her disturbance.

5. *Cherchez le should, cherchez le must—look for the should, look for the must!* With this slogan, Ellis exhorts clients to identify and dispute the irrational beliefs which are at the core of their upsets.

6. *There are no fucking musts in the universe!* From the RET perspective, it is impossible to find logical or empirical support for the existence of absolute shoulds, musts, and have to's.

There are, of course, numerous other memorable phrases which Ellis liberally sprinkles throughout his therapy sessions. These phrases summarize important elements of rational-emotive philosophy and therapy, and may be the most salient features of the therapeutic process for many clients. Even when given clients are too dull, unmotivated, or disorganized to become effective disputers of irrational beliefs, they may be able to attain some degree of symptomatic relief merely by thinking about and repeating Ellis's slogans to themselves.

CAN PSYCHOTHERAPY CLIENTS TRULY ATTAIN A RATIONAL PHILOSOPHY?

Ellis (1976) has noted that biologically based traits are difficult to modify. His clinical observations have led him to believe that human beings easily tend to engage in irrational thinking, and he views this tendency as having primarily a biological basis (Ellis, 1976, 1977b, 1979a, 1987b). As such, he takes the position that this tendency is difficult to alter, and that it is largely ineradicable.

In culling through his various writings on this issue, it appears Ellis has concluded that the vast majority of human beings can to varying degrees approach, but not attain, a complete, pervasive, and enduring rational phi-losophy of life.[2] Further, for most psychotherapy clients, merely approach-ing such a goal requires an immense amount of self-discipline and prolonged effort. This state of affairs represents something of a catch-22 situation, as many psychotherapy clients enter therapy with what Ellis would describe as abysmally low frustration tolerance. Even for clients who are able to make above-average efforts, periodic backsliding is regarded as inevitable (Ellis, 1984a, 1985a).

To make a gloomy picture even gloomier, Ellis (1983a, 1987b) has described the following factors as additional obstacles to helping individuals replace their self-defeating philosophies with a more functional one:

1. *Demands for quick relief*: Most people tend to be attracted to quick and easy methods of resolving their emotional distress. These methods are likely to bring only temporary relief, however, and distract individuals from working at the types of philosophical changes most likely to provide lasting benefits.

2. *Changing circumstances*: Unfortunate conditions (i.e., activating events) can serve as the initial impetus for emotional disturbance. These activating events may fortuitously change for the better, discouraging some people from entering therapy and encouraging others to terminate prematurely.

3. *Secondary disturbances*: Not only do human beings create their primary emotional disturbances, they also create secondary disturbances for them-selves by thinking irrationally about their primary symptoms. These sec-ondary disturbances increase the complexity and difficulty involved in becoming symptom-free.

4. *Subtle irrationalities*: Most people—especially those who tend to be "difficult customers" in psychotherapy—hold both blatant and subtle irra-tional beliefs. The subtle irrational beliefs are more difficult for both client and therapist to identify, and thus more difficult to dispute.

5. *Reinforcement of irrational thinking*: The emotional and behavioral ef-fects of holding certain irrational beliefs can sometimes result in reinforcing consequences, which serve to augment the degree to which the individual subscribes to these beliefs. As an example, the irrational belief that "Others *must* treat me fairly" can lead to anger and aggressive behavior, which in turn may cause a favorable modification in the way one is treated by certain others. Angry behavior is thus reinforced, and the belief behind it is strengthened.

6. *Hopelessness*: When individuals have had particular emotional and be-havioral problems for a long period of time, they may erroneously conclude that these difficulties are unmodifiable. This would tend to discourage them from entering or working at therapy.

7. *Other cognitive factors*: Ignorance, intellectual dullness, unperceptive-

ness, and defensiveness also represent significant obstacles to making deep philosophical changes.

Despite the large number of variables which increase the difficulty of changing one's basic philosophy of life, Ellis (1987b) has described himself as optimistic about the prospects of achieving sound mental health. He believes, after all, that human beings possess considerable self-actualizing tendencies as well as a predisposition to think and act in a self defeating manner (Dryden & Ellis, 1986; Ellis, 1962, 1987b). In addition, he sees various ways in which psychotherapy in general and RET in particular can be refined (Ellis, 1982, 1983a, 1985a, 1987a; Bernard, 1986). Finally, he looks forward to a day when the tenets of rational living will routinely be taught in schools and other major institutions, as well as effectively conveyed through the mass media. In his view, early and consistent exposure to this material may well help human beings to combat their innate tendencies to think irrationally.

NOTES

1. Rational-emotive therapy (RET) was originally named rational therapy (RT).
2. Ellis (Weinrach & Ellis, 1980) has acknowledged his own limitations in this regard. While he describes himself as being "superelegant" in the sense that he almost never causes himself to experience anxiety or depression, he notes that he has had to work at overcoming a tendency towards anger and irritability. He admits that he still occasionally experiences these feelings.

7

Assessing Progress and Preparing for Termination

My main goals in treating any of my psychotherapy clients are simple and concrete: To leave patients, at the end of the psychotherapeutic process, with a minimum of anxiety (or self-blame) and of hostility (or blame of others and the world around them); and, just as importantly, to give them a method of self-observation and self-assessment that will ensure that, for the rest of their lives, they continue to be minimally anxious and hostile. (Ellis, 1967, p. 207)

RET attempts to provide clients with techniques and strategies which they can use to independently overcome their behavioral problems and emotional disturbance. In this sense, it can be viewed as preparing clients for termination from the very onset of treatment. It focuses on helping clients to "become their own therapists," and both directly and indirectly discourages the formation of a dependent relationship with the practitioner.

Aside from teaching clients a set of useful techniques, RET contains certain emphases which further serve to facilitate movement towards successful termination. Clients are encouraged, for instance, to accept responsibility for creating and maintaining their emotional disturbance, rather than blaming it upon unfortunate aspects of their past history or current circumstances. In addition, the regular and consistent use of homework assignments within RET conveys the message that change-oriented activities outside of therapy sessions are at least as important as the weekly verbal exchanges between client and therapist. Finally, RET places an emphasis upon hard work—clients are taught that the probability of approaching emotional adjustment and self-actualization is greatly enhanced by their willingness to face their difficulties and expend personal effort in utilizing RET techniques.

Despite the fact that the content and process of RET seem oriented towards termination, Ellis has written very little about termination issues. Likewise, it proved difficult to cull termination material from the audiotapes of Ellis's sessions which form the basis for this book. While Ellis could frequently be heard offering encouragement to clients and praising their efforts at working to resolve their problems, he rarely spoke specifically about ending the therapeutic relationship. Whether this was due simply to a non-representative sampling of tapes or to Ellis's particular approach to therapy was initially unclear; nevertheless, it proved impossible to identify any particular recording as representing a definite "termination session."

This paucity of material created a quandary for the authors of this volume in terms of finding a vehicle which would provide an accurate portrayal of Ellis's approach to termination issues. It was finally decided to go right to the source: The current chapter presents an interview which one of the authors (J.Y.) conducted with Ellis. This interview serves to illuminate his position on termination criteria, client dependence, post-treatment expectancies, and several other pertinent issues.

TERMINATION ISSUES:
AN INTERVIEW WITH ALBERT ELLIS

YANKURA: What are your criteria for successful therapy? In other words, how do you know when a given client is ready for termination?

ELLIS: One obvious criterion—although perhaps not a very good one—is that the client no longer has the specific problem with which he or she entered therapy. A male client may become better able to get or maintain an erection, for example, so that's relatively clear cut. I'm not certain, however, that there are many situations that are so clear cut.

YANKURA: What other criteria might you employ to assess a client's readiness for termination?

ELLIS: I may notice that particular clients are coming into sessions and reporting fewer failures and more successes. Here, I'm referring to cases in which clients have worked at therapy to the point where virtually nothing is shameful or embarrassing to them, and where they're rarely getting themselves anxious about anything. They're dealing fairly well with any problems that arise, and when they feel even temporarily depressed or anxious they manage to overcome it pretty quickly by using their RET skills. They may then have relatively little to discuss with me—some may even leave before their half-hour session is over! We may then decide to decrease the frequency of the sessions, until *they* finally suggest that we leave off for the time being. They know that they can always return to therapy if they wish.

YANKURA: You stated that clients will report more frequent successes and fewer failures. Do you take steps to determine whether the progress they are reporting is genuine?

ELLIS: Yes—I listen carefully to their spontaneous reports, and I tend to adopt a somewhat suspicious stance. Clients will often tell me, for example, that they are doing much better—meaning that they're no longer experiencing significant anxiety or depression. I might respond to this by saying, "*This* time you weren't anxious or depressed—because you succeeded at the goal you wanted to achieve! What would have happened if you *hadn't* succeeded?" They may then acknowledge that if they had really fallen on their faces and had done poorly, they probably would have gone back to feeling anxious and depressed. So, I listen to their spontaneous reports and try to determine whether they're genuinely improving—they may be *feeling* better, but they may not actually be *getting* better.

I also frequently suspect that the improvements they report are not consistent and pervasive. They may indeed be doing better with regard to the problem with which they originally entered therapy, but they may not be doing much in terms of using RET to improve their other areas of functioning. I will check on them fairly often in a variety of ways, including monitoring their progress with homework assignments. They might, for example, report that they're no longer socially anxious, but I may find that they're still not doing much dating.

YANKURA: Can you provide an example of a case in which you used homework to check on the client's progress?

ELLIS: Yes—here's an example: One of my group clients really worked at his approval anxiety for three or four months, seemed to get better, and then terminated his participation in the group. He returned several months later because his woman friend wanted therapy, and she initially wouldn't come to the group sessions without him. At the point at which he re-entered the group, he claimed that he no longer got himself feeling ashamed about anything, because he had learned how to use RET. Nevertheless, the co-therapists and I decided to give him a shame-attacking exercise in order to check the validity of his report. You see, over the years I've had a number of clients who stated they were no longer ashamed to do certain things, when in reality this wasn't true.

So, this particular client agreed to do one of our more famous shame-attacking exercises: He took a potted plant, decorated it with condoms, and hung a big sign on it that said "rubber tree." He then carried it with him on the subway during rush hour, and had no difficulty doing it. His woman friend sat far away from him, however, because *she* was ashamed—she didn't want to be identified with him! But *he* seemed to have done quite okay, at least in terms of overcoming feelings of shame.

YANKURA: This particular client terminated therapy when he perceived that he had made progress in overcoming his emotional disturbance. Do you find that many clients will quit therapy before having reached such a point?

ELLIS: Yes—clients will often quit therapy for many "pseudo-reasons," before they're really ready for termination. They may, for example, enter therapy because they've been unable to find a good mate—and then, perhaps serendipitously, they meet one. At that point they may choose to terminate, even though their basic emotional problems haven't really been resolved. Either partly by design or by accident, they managed to find a good partner—and incidentally, there's no way of knowing whether that partner is going to *remain* a good choice. But people will frequently leave therapy for such reasons— their unfortunate circumstances or activating events have fortuitously changed for the better. That doesn't mean, however, that they've really worked at solving their emotional problems.

Clients will also sometimes quit because the therapy is getting "too close for comfort"—it's bringing up problems and provoking feelings that they don't really want to deal with. A good number probably leave therapy because they believe their therapist has antagonized them in some fashion or another. Now, the therapist may truly have treated them poorly, or may have done just one thing which they consider very wrong. Even though the therapist might have been of considerable further assistance to them, they decide to quit.

Another reason that clients may quit is because they perceive that they've made practically no improvement, and they believe that they're wasting their time. They may erroneously believe that RET is not for them, and their friends may talk them into trying a new kind of therapy or a different therapist. It might have been possible for them to discuss and resolve these issues with their therapist, but they simply don't bother.

It's probably the case, however, that most clients who quit therapy are *feeling* better. Of course, there's no way of knowing for certain whether that change will be temporary or permanent. Innumerable people terminate therapy prematurely, later acknowledge it, and return to therapy a year or two down the road.

YANKURA: Are there any particular aspects of RET that promote premature termination?

ELLIS: It's fairly easy for a competent therapist to teach most clients the basic principles and techniques of RET. As a result, clients may become able to apply RET on their own within a relatively brief span of treatment time, and may believe that it's appropriate to terminate. In many cases, however, they may not be using RET's techniques as much as they could—hence, they're not deriving the full benefits.

Another reason that clients may terminate RET prematurely is because the therapy gets boring—the same kind of thing may be gone over again and again. Also, RET pushes clients to *work* at overcoming their problems—not just to understand themselves creatively, which may be enjoyable. Clients with low frustration tolerance may want to avoid the hard work which RET advocates, so they may quit.

YANKURA: In your view, what is the most appropriate reason for clients to terminate?

ELLIS: The best reason for clients to quit is that they're achieving the elegant solution. Their original presenting problem—let's say it was some specific anxiety—has largely been resolved, and they've explored aspects of the anxiety other than those of which they were originally aware. Their general tendency towards anxiety is thus much improved, and they've reached a point where they rarely make themselves anxious about anything. When they *do* cause themselves to become anxious, they quickly utilize their disputing skills and get relieved.

That's an example of attaining the elegant solution, but I'm not sure that many clients terminate for that reason. Some of them may attain it *after* their formal therapy contacts have ended—they're aware that they've improved during the course of therapy, and they decide that they want to continue working towards the elegant solution on their own. That's quite legitimate. Nevertheless, I think that many people quit therapy when they're only partially solving their emotional problems—it's possible that they could do a lot better.

YANKURA: Can you describe one particular case that you regard as a successful termination? More specifically, can you recall a client who made progress with his or her original presenting problems *and* made steps towards approaching the elegant solution?

ELLIS: I recall one client who originally came for a sex problem. He had retarded ejaculation, and would also frequently lose his erections and not ejaculate at all. He first had several individual sessions with me, and later became a member of one of my groups. After perhaps a couple of months of RET, he had definitely conquered his sexual problems.

As he continued in therapy, however, he realized that his major problem was negative self-rating. He became able to see that it was adversely affecting his work performance, as well as his intimate and social relationships. Once he saw this, he started to work his ass off in order to overcome it. He kept raising it as an issue in the group, and by the time he stopped therapy he was in quite good shape with regard to feelings of worth—he had reached the point where he rarely put himself down. He generalized—in the sense of using RET to effect positive changes in a number of areas—and derived greater benefit from therapy than he had first anticipated.

When clients go further than their original presenting problem and get to the point where they rarely upset themselves about *anything*, it's because—in RET terms—they've made a profound philosophic change. They've gone beyond merely working against the symptom.

YANKURA: The individual you've just described broadened his focus during therapy and was able to work on modifying fundamental aspects of his personal philosophy. Do you find that this frequently occurs with the clients you see?

ELLIS: I have many people who enter therapy with vocational, school, or relationship problems, and then realize that their difficulties are largely connected with ego anxiety and feelings of worthlessness. They may then start working on these issues, such that they're able to make broader and more deep-seated improvements.

YANKURA: Do clients generally become aware of these broader issues on their own, or do you actively point them out?

ELLIS: I actively point them out, although in group therapy they're able to listen to other clients' problems and may sometimes realize that they have similar difficulties.

Because I've written so many books on sexual problems, many clients will come to see me believing that their difficulties are strictly limited to their sexual functioning. That, however, is often not the case. To illustrate, I have a relatively new client who entered therapy with specific complaints concerning impotence. I explained to him that in all probability he's overfocusing on intercourse, and sacredizing it. He tended to deny this at first, but as we went on he began to acknowledge that I was probably correct. He also started to see that he also has the *general* problem of self-deprecation: When he doesn't do well in a given area, he puts himself down. If he decides to continue in therapy, he'll probably more readily admit to his general anxiety and will work to overcome it.

YANKURA: My impression is that you generally allow clients to arrive at their own decisions regarding when to terminate. Are there occasions when you will be more directive with regard to this issue?

ELLIS: That's *usually* not my approach. If, however, I see that they're consistently coming in to sessions with relatively little to talk about, I might suggest reducing the frequency of the sessions. Or we might both decide that they have little to discuss and are doing very well, and agree that they'll return if and when they want to. Some do return later, but many I never see again.

YANKURA: Are there any other circumstances that might lead you to terminate a given client? As a former co-leader of your groups, for instance, I can recall occasions when you would recommend that a particular client had better quit for a while.

ELLIS: That's right. Once in a while I'll point out to the DC's—the difficult customers—that they're not doing much in terms of completing homework assignments and working on their problems, and that we're probably wasting time. I might give them an assignment—such as dating ten women or going for twenty job interviews—and suggest that they not return to group until they've done it. I try to make it clear to them that they're probably not going to improve if they just return each week and keep repeating the same thing over and over. So occasionally—though not very often—I sort of get rid of them *until* they do some homework.

Now, I might also have some psychotic clients whom I think might be disruptive or potentially dangerous to the group—I'll try to get them out of group and into individual therapy. With other individuals I may say, "I'm not going to meet with you until you see about getting some medication," because it's apparent that their psychosis makes them less receptive to the therapy. Occasionally I may suggest hospitalization, especially for drug-addicted clients. The same may apply to psychotic clients who had best be stabilized in a hospital setting.

YANKURA: At this point I would like to shift the focus of the interview to consideration of ways in which you might prepare clients to function independently after therapy is over. First, what steps do you take to prevent your clients from becoming dependent on you?

ELLIS: I don't give them love, so they usually don't become enamored of me. A few of the females may, but that's much less frequent now that I'm older. At this point, in fact, those few females have tended to be older women!

I give my clients help and support, but I try to show them that in many respects I'm really a problem-solver—not just a nice listener. As such, I'm frequently pushing them to *do* something to resolve their problems, particularly with regard to activities they can undertake independently outside of the therapy sessions. If clients seem to go for my approval and hesitate to speak openly with me, I raise that as an issue—I show them that they don't *need* my approval.

Now, it's important to recognize that some forms of dependency may be therapeutically acceptable. A number of clients, such as schizophrenics, tend to function inadequately in many respects. Such clients may require pushing, advice-giving, and problem-solving for a long, long time. As a result, the therapeutic relationship may be likely to continue for quite a while. Would you refer to that as dependency in the negative sense of the term, or could you call it "therapeutic dependency"?

Overall, I would guess that my clients are distinctly less dependent on me than they are on other types of therapists. I don't know if they become more dependent on *other* RETers—other RETers may *like* dependency and give their clients more warmth and love than I do, in combination with the RET.

YANKURA: Do you take explicit steps to have clients attribute positive changes to their own efforts, rather than to some "magic" you affected during the therapy?

ELLIS: I will frequently address their perceptions with regard to that issue. They may say, for example, "You got me to change, *you* helped me." In response I say, "Yes, that's partly true, but don't forget that *you* pushed your ass. You took what I said and used it to overcome your problems." I attempt to get them to see as much as possible that they don't *need* me. I think that it can be very therapeutic to give them the impression that they're able to make it on their own—when, indeed, they are. If they're in that minority group I spoke about a moment ago and are going to require therapeutic support for a long time, I may not do that.

YANKURA: In terms of clients' post-treatment expectancies, do you deal with the possibility that they might place unreasonable demands on themselves regarding their independent use of RET?

ELLIS: Yes, I will sometimes warn them about that. More specifically, I tell them not to expect that RET will rid them of appropriate negative emotions such as sadness, regret, frustration, et cetera. Also, I tell them not to expect that they'll never fall back. Otherwise, they may become disillusioned with RET.

YANKURA: Would you say that with most clients you make a point of teaching about the limitations of human beings with regard to rational thinking?

ELLIS: I go through that in one way or another with most clients. With some, I do it at the very beginning of therapy. I tell them that they can expect to fall on their faces fairly often, and that all humans are out of their minds simply because they're human. By the time they quit therapy, they're hopefully able to see that there's just no way in which they can be perfectly adjusted and never experience emotional disturbance!

YANKURA: What other advice might you offer to terminating clients?

ELLIS: Years ago, I used to suggest to clients that they would do well to return for a yearly check-up. I found that few did, however, so I stopped suggesting it—but I still think it's probably a good idea.

YANKURA: What would you hope to accomplish during those check-up sessions?

ELLIS: I would try to determine whether or not clients had fallen back. At first, they might not even be aware of it themselves—but with questioning and confrontation they could be helped to recognize it. I would systematically review the social, sexual, and vocational aspects of their functioning, and see if they're making attempts to work towards self-actualization. The ideal is not just to help clients overcome their disturbance, but also to help them lead a happier, better life. It would be preferable if people were able to add to their sense of fulfillment and pleasure in life, rather than merely leading a rather mundane—though relatively undisturbed—existence.

CONCLUDING COMMENTS

In reviewing the text of this interview, the reasons for the previously-mentioned difficulty in identifying a termination audiotape become more apparent: By his own report, Ellis does not typically broach the issue of termination with clients—he usually waits for them to "suggest that we leave off for the time being." This, of course, is not an inviolable rule, for Ellis is sensitive to signs that the client is making progress in therapy. He will take note of the fact that the individual has less to talk about during therapy sessions, is less frequently upsetting him or her self, and is reporting more successes than failures with regard to dealing with difficult or unfortunate activating events. When these signs are present, he may himself suggest that the therapy sessions decrease in frequency.

At first glance, it might appear odd that Ellis adopts this seemingly laissez faire approach to therapy termination. After all, his reputation as a therapist is based at least partly on his exceptionally active-directive stance within sessions. It is likely, however, that his manner of approaching termination is related to his position on the ability of human beings to attain the profound philosophic changes advocated by RET. Such change is viewed as quite difficult to approach, even when clients are willing to devote considerable time and effort to working towards it. As such, Ellis may be willing to serve as an instigator and guide on the road to rationality as long as it appears that the client is making efforts to reach this destination.

PART II
SPECIAL ISSUES

8

Efficiency and Force in Psychotherapy

I was born with a gene for efficiency, while Freud was probably born with a gene for inefficiency. (From introductory remarks made by Albert Ellis at one of his Friday night workshops, "Problems of Daily Living.")

In many of his writings, Ellis has stressed the importance of therapists conveying rational beliefs to clients in a vigorous, forceful, and dramatic manner (see, for example, Ellis, 1979c). As clients often rigidly subscribe to the irrational beliefs behind their emotional and behavioral problems, therapists are strongly advised to attack these beliefs by being quite active and directive during therapy sessions. Such an approach is deemed most likely to contribute to beneficial changes for clients, and is hence viewed as a key element in conducting effective psychotherapy.

Ellis practices what he (non-dogmatically!) preaches in this regard, as evidenced by the published reports of researchers who have subjected recordings of his psychotherapy sessions to content analyses. Becker and Rosenfeld (1976), for example, studied twenty audiotape recordings of Ellis's initial sessions with clients. They found that a large portion of his statements during these sessions consisted of didactic teaching, rhetorical (as compared to factual) questions, the use of concrete examples as a teaching tool, directly describing the nature of an irrational belief held by a client, and logical arguments against irrational beliefs. In a study which compared the verbal behaviors of Rogers, Perls, and Ellis in the film, *Three Approaches to Psychotherapy* (Shostrum, 1966),[1] Hill, Thames, and Rardin (1979) found that Ellis primarily made use of information giving and direct guidance in his work with a volunteer "client." Significantly, they also noted that he was the most verbally-active of the three therapists, which they found to be appropriate to his "reeducative rather than exploratory stance" within psychotherapy.

In reviewing the collection of audiotaped sessions which form the basis for this book, it was noted that Ellis engages in a number of verbal behaviors (other than those listed above) which can be considered characteristic of the manner in which he translates the terms force and energy into actual clinical practice. These behaviors can be considered to fall into the following categories:[2]

Profanity

Ellis frequently employs what he has referred to as "the sprightly use of obscenity" (Ellis, 1977c) in his work with clients. His use of impious language serves as a vehicle for emphasizing particular points that he wishes to make, as well as a means for breaking down the barriers to intimacy which might exist between a client and a therapist. With regard to the latter effect, it is noted that most individuals may be likely to limit their use of profanity to interactions with their closest associates.

Repetition

Ellis will often repeat particular messages that he wishes to convey to a given client, thus increasing the probability that the content of the message (e.g., a rational belief that can serve to replace a specific irrational belief) will be acquired. In addition to repetition of specific messages, he will also repeat his coverage of more global issues of relevance to the client. As an example, he might review the possible causes and manifestations of a client's approval anxiety across several sessions. Such repetition stems from his recognition that individuals will frequently fail to internalize information upon its first presentation.

Persistence

Ellis will persist in his attempts at disputing particular irrational beliefs within sessions until he has obtained some evidence that the client is (a) disputing these beliefs on his or her own, and (b) making some progress in replacing them with a more rational perspective.

Directive Stance

Ellis typically does not follow the flow of the client's verbalizations during sessions; rather, he is quite active in leading the client to focus on particular problem areas from the very beginning of therapy. On occasion he will encounter a client who seems to compulsively jump from topic to topic, but even in such cases it is usually apparent that his questions and comments are intended to assist the individual in concentrating upon the identification and resolution of some specific problem.

Confrontation/Insistence

Clients will often adopt a defensive stance during therapy sessions, such that they deny or minimize the significance of particular emotional and behavioral problems. In addition, they will sometimes take a "helpless" position, wherein they appear to insist that they are unable to think through to a solution of their difficulties. Ellis will be quite confrontational on both counts, in terms of presenting clients with strong evidence for the existence of specific problems and their ability to work effectively towards problem-resolution.

Ellis is concerned with obtaining effective results in his psychotherapy, in the sense of assisting clients in the process of obtaining relief from their original presenting symptoms. He is, however, also interested in increasing the *efficiency* of treatment, with regard to the amount of time and effort required to achieve genuinely effective outcomes. In a number of his publications (Ellis, 1980b; 1982) he has detailed what he considers to be the characteristics of efficient psychotherapy:

1. Brevity: Efficient psychotherapy often obtains effective results within a relatively brief span of treatment time.

2. Depth-Centeredness: Efficient treatment identifies the underlying "causes" (i.e., irrational belief systems) of a client's dysfunctional emotions and behaviors and is able to help the client work at minimizing their disruptive impact.

3. Pervasiveness: The therapy process assists clients in identifying and dealing with *many* of their emotional and behavioral problems, rather than focusing exclusively upon presenting symptoms.

4. Extensiveness: Efficient psychotherapy helps clients not only to overcome their inappropriate negative emotions, but also to approach self-actualization and maximize their potential for happier living.

5. Thoroughgoingness: The treatment process is not overly dependent upon one type of technique or strategy, but incorporates a variety of therapeutic techniques in the service of assisting clients to make beneficial modifications in their thoughts, feelings, and behaviors.

6. A Focus on Maintenance of Progress: Not only are clients improved at the end of treatment; they are able to maintain and add to this improvement after therapy has been terminated.

7. A Focus on Prevention: Clients have acquired a philosophy and a set of skills by treatment's end which will enable them to avoid the development of future emotional and behavioral dysfunctions.

In addition to the above criteria, Ellis (1980b) has also written that efficient psychotherapy incorporates concepts and techniques which are easily understood by clients, and which can easily be taught to therapists-in-training. He notes that it is desirable for a psychotherapeutic system to be intrinsically interesting for both client and therapist, and for clients to be able to derive maximum benefits from its ministrations with minimal harm to themselves and others. Finally, efficient psychotherapy tends to be flexible and non-dogmatic, and is devised in such a way that its theories can be validated (or refuted) through controlled scientific inquiry.

This chapter will present a transcript of a therapy session which will serve to illustrate the manner in which Ellis conducts forceful and efficient psychotherapy. In addition, this transcript will be used to highlight the previously-listed array of behaviors which can be considered characteristic of the manner in which Ellis applies force and energy in his clinical practice.

FORCE AND EFFICIENCY IN PRACTICE: AN ILLUSTRATIVE SESSION

In the following transcript, Ellis works with an unemployed middle-aged female client who is assiduously avoiding the task of job-hunting. It is apparent that this session is not the client's first exposure to RET, as she makes statements which indicate some degree of familiarity with Ellis's writings and approach. Nevertheless, it appears that she is a novice at applying rational-emotive concepts and techniques to the resolution of her problem areas. The session begins with the client making a specific request for some assistance in overcoming her task-avoidance:

CLIENT: I was reading *A New Guide to Rational Living* again, and two chapters in it were very helpful to me—the chapters on self-discipline and getting rid of inertia. I'm looking for a job, and I want to see if I can get some extra help in getting off of my ass.

ELLIS: All right—what's blocking you from getting off your ass?

CLIENT: I'm scared!

ELLIS: Avoid using a word like "scared"—it's too vague. Now, see if you can answer this question: "If I got off my ass and went out into the world . . . ," what might happen?

CLIENT: (Pause) Well, I think it's just habit. I've never done it before.

ELLIS: It's not just habit! You're probably inert because of low frustration tolerance. But let's keep on the "scared" part for a moment—what are you afraid of? Forget about "habit" for the time being—we'll get back to that later.

CLIENT: I don't really know if I'm scared. I'm just guessing that I am.

ELLIS: Then why'd you say that? You must have some indication that you're scared . . .

CLIENT: I'm either scared, or else I think the world owes me a living.

ELLIS: Let's start with the "scared." Those two things are not the same.

CLIENT: Well, I once heard someone tell a story about a little animal that was peeking out of its hole because it was hungry. It was hungry, but it was too scared to come out—so it finally starved to death, peeking out of its hole. I sort of identify with that animal, so that's what makes me think I'm scared.

ELLIS: I think that you *are* scared. I don't doubt that you have the other thing— the low frustration tolerance—which we'll get back to, but let's just stick to the anxiety, the scariness. *What* is scary?

CLIENT: I think I'm scared about job-hunting because I've never done it before.

ELLIS: That's not true—there are millions of things you've never done before. If I gave you a million dollars and told you to go to the Kentucky Derby— which presumably you've never done—would you be scared of going?

CLIENT: Well, not really. Not like this.

ELLIS: Right. There are a lot of things you wouldn't be scared of—which are much more frightening than looking for a job. If you've never skied, for example, and again you had plenty of money—and I said, "Go ski- ing," you probably would go skiing—even though there really *is* danger involved. So, you're not scared just because you've never done it be- fore—you're scared of something more concrete. Now, think about it— don't give up! If you don't get beyond merely recognizing that you're scared, you'll never solve the problem. What would you really be afraid of if you went out day after day and pushed to find a job?

Less than ten minutes into this session, Ellis has already accomplished several important therapeutic tasks. He has begun to make a distinction between ego anxiety and discomfort anxiety[3] (without explicitly employ- ing these terms), and has rather forcefully directed the client to examine her "anxiety" before jumping to consideration of her low frustration tolerance. In addition, he has encouraged the client to become specific with regard to the nature of her anxiety ("Avoid using a word like 'scared'—it's too vague."), and has presented a logical argument to counter her view that it stems merely from a lack of experience with the behaviors involved in seeking employment. This intervention can be viewed as operating in the service of a depth-centered approach, as Ellis uses it to help the client get at the beliefs behind her anxiety.

CLIENT: Oh, Dr. Ellis! (Pause) Well, what are most people afraid of?

ELLIS: I know the answer to that question—but first let's see if *you* can figure out what *you're* afraid of.

CLIENT: Do you think it's because I'm afraid I can't do it, that I won't get hired? I'm afraid that someone won't grab me on my first try, and then I'll think I'm . . .

ELLIS: You'll think you're what?

CLIENT: I'll think maybe . . . that someone out there isn't all excited about having the Queen of the May come to work for them. That I'll then think I'm worthless . . .

ELLIS: Right—but think that through—don't just say it because you think that it might apply to other people. Think about what would really occur in your *gut* if you went out for twenty or thirty job interviews and they all didn't want you. How would you tend to feel?

CLIENT: I think I'd just be completely passive like many women; that it's just something new. But you don't agree . . .

ELLIS: No—that's a falsehood! Unless you face things, you're not going to solve them! That's an easy way to cover up! And as I said before, we'll get back to that other thing later—that's a different feeling. Let's stick to the anxiety.

CLIENT: (Musing to self) Why am I scared? Why am I scared to go out and get a job? (To Ellis) I'm scared I'll be turned down—but why should I be scared about that?

ELLIS: Because . . . how would you feel if twenty or thirty times in a row . . .

CLIENT: . . . And I'll think, "Here I am, a middle-aged woman turned down," . . . and then I'd just get to feeling worse and worse.

ELLIS: Because you'd be concluding what? What would be your conclusion?

CLIENT: That nobody wants me.

ELLIS: And that would be . . . ?

CLIENT: That would be terrible.

ELLIS: All right—now, did you just *say* that, or do you believe that that would probably occur?

CLIENT: I just don't know!

ELLIS: Well, think about it! You're avoiding thinking about it. I would know perfectly well, for example, how I would feel if I got turned down for thirty jobs.

CLIENT: Of course I'd feel very upset!

ELLIS: Well, what would the upsetness be?

CLIENT: The upsetness would be that there's something wrong with *me*!

ELLIS: And that that's *awful*.

CLIENT: Right.

Through confrontation/insistence, Ellis encourages the client to make an effort at examining her own thoughts and feelings, rather than adopting a helpless stance or merely responding to his questions with what she believes to be the "right" answers. He again refocuses her to the issue at hand, and helps her to begin gaining some insight as to the negative self-rating issues which underlie her anxiety.

ELLIS: But why would those be two nutty conclusions?

CLIENT: Because working would be better than sitting home—that's awful, too!

ELLIS: No, that's not the reason. You see, you're not zeroing in—you're not using your head.

CLIENT: The obvious answer is that I would probably be getting turned down for economic reasons.

ELLIS: That's right—it *doesn't* prove that there's something *wrong* with you! These are lousy times, and there are relatively few jobs available.

CLIENT: Yeah—but you know, I remember now . . . all of my life, I've never gone out and gotten a job—I've never gone out and done one thing! I just waited 'till something happened.

ELLIS: Because, "If I stuck my neck out . . ."

CLIENT: I might find out that . . .

ELLIS: What?

CLIENT: I wasn't any good!

ELLIS: Right—"I would *conclude* that I wasn't any good." You see, you *wouldn't* find out that you weren't any good—that's practically impossible.

CLIENT: It has nothing to do with being middle-aged now, because I was that same way when I was nineteen.

ELLIS: Yeah—but you remind me that at seventeen or eighteen I would never go out and look for a job—because I would be so afraid of rejection!

CLIENT: (Surprised) *You?*

ELLIS: That's right! But at nineteen I started getting over it—today, I have infinitely *less* anxiety.

CLIENT: You have less today?

ELLIS: Yes—because I've worked against my anxiety, and you never have!

CLIENT: Mm-hm.

ELLIS: So I think you're quite right—it has very little to do with your age. The chances of your getting rejections may have increased—but that's not necessarily true! Lots of women your age are considered highly desirable as employees, while many times the younger ones aren't.

(A discussion as to the reasons that an older woman may be preferred by some employers occurs here. It is omitted for the sake of brevity.)

CLIENT: Well now, I get mixed up when I read your book—because I see so many things to be working on.

ELLIS: But you're moving from one thing to another! Now, stick to the anxiety—you're going to get mixed up if you keep jumping around and using one as an excuse for another. You'd better face the fact—which we've just barely gotten into—that you've always been scared shitless of rejection.

CLIENT: So, the same thing would apply to making new friends, new boyfriends, everything! I still *wait*—wait for it to come to me!

ELLIS: That's right. Your passivity is not *merely* laziness—although I'm not saying that that's not an element that's involved . . .

CLIENT: No . . . but it is laziness, too . . . and being spoiled as a child.

ELLIS: It's not "being spoiled"! That has practically nothing to do with it! That's just a cop out.

CLIENT: Really?

ELLIS: Well, Nelson Rockefeller was spoiled!

CLIENT: Right, right.

ELLIS: He never had to do one day's work in his life—but as far as I know, Rocky always worked his ass off!

CLIENT: Well, I don't mean spoiled—I mean . . . well, you know . . . no discipline, or anything—not trained . . .

ELLIS: But we don't know that Rockefeller got any discipline. It's a little unlikely that he got *much*, because he was probably raised by nurses—and they're not going to discipline a child who has ten million dollars!

Ellis begins this portion of the transcript by asking a question which is intended to prompt the client into seeing the erroneous nature of the meanings she attaches to rejection experiences. When she responds in an irrelevant fashion, he quickly intervenes and again insists that she "use her head."

When the client makes reference to childhood experiences ("being spoiled") as being responsible for her current passivity, Ellis moves in with a strong dispute by citing the example of Nelson Rockefeller. The response he makes here is quite important, as it serves to illustrate that "A" doesn't cause "C" and encourages the client to take responsibility for her problems. It is possible that this intervention serves its purpose, as the client moves into new territory:

CLIENT: Well, then—what do I say to myself about rejection and all of these different things? Not just jobs, but . . .

ELLIS: Well, what *are* you saying to yourself? Because as I said, you'd better vividly picture yourself trying for twenty or thirty jobs, and getting rejected for various reasons.

CLIENT: You mean you want me to definitely picture that.

ELLIS: That's right.

CLIENT: And then picture my reaction?

ELLIS: That's right—what your feeling would be and what you would be saying to yourself to create that feeling.

CLIENT: You want me to do that now? Picture that?

ELLIS: Yeah—picture it and see what you're feeling in your gut, as you get rejected for the twentieth time.

CLIENT: Well, I know that I must be planning to go out and look for a job, because for the last few weeks I've had a feeling in my gut of such anxiety and nervousness . . .

ELLIS: So there's your answer. Now, what do you think you'd be telling yourself—and don't just give me an answer from my book—what do you think *you* would be telling yourself?

CLIENT: I'm telling myself that I'm going to do it.

ELLIS: "And if I do it . . ."

CLIENT: It's going to be hell, it's going to be like jumping into a pot of boiling water or something . . .

ELLIS: Because . . . ?

CLIENT: Because I guess I think I'm going to be rejected.

ELLIS: And that would mean . . . ?

CLIENT: Or else I think I'm going to be . . . you know, it's a mixture of grandiose thoughts . . .

ELLIS: Well, wait a minute—first stick with this one: "If I got rejected, that would mean . . . "

CLIENT: That would mean that I'm right about myself.

ELLIS: "That I'm really no good." Is that what you're saying?

CLIENT: Yeah.

The client begins this section by displaying her awareness of the desirability of generating an alternative philosophy to deal with rejection experiences, but again evinces helplessness by asking, ". . . what do I say to myself . . . ?" Ellis responds by turning her question back at her, thus creating an opportunity to uncover her current dysfunctional beliefs. His directive to ". . . vividly picture yourself . . . getting rejected for various reasons" can be considered an example of thoroughgoingness in therapy (i.e., increasing efficiency by employing a variety of techniques), as he is attempting to prompt the client to use imagery as a vehicle for gaining insights into her irrational beliefs. The non-verbal cognitive content of an imagery experience can be seen to deviate considerably from the verbally-loaded interventions which Ellis mainly employs, and adds a multi-modal tone to the session.

Following the imagery directive, Ellis utilizes a series of "incomplete sentences" (e.g., "And that would mean . . . ?") to direct the client to her irrational conclusions regarding her worth in the face of rejections. This technique appears to be favored by Ellis, as he can be heard using it in a majority of his sessions.

ELLIS: All right—now let's look at the other side for a moment. Let's suppose you picture getting *accepted*.

CLIENT: Then I'd manage to say it must be a lousy job or something.

ELLIS: What else would you say? Let's suppose you got interviewed a few times, and your fifth or sixth time out they say to you, "Well, you seem to be the one we want—we want a woman around your age, because we'd like her to stay, and it looks like you can handle this job." So they've accepted you. Now, you're about to go into work on Monday . . .

CLIENT: Yeah—well, I wouldn't mind that as much, because I'd be over the main hurdle. I'd be quite nervous about it, but . . .

ELLIS: Because . . . ? Wait a minute, you'd better not run over that quickly. You see, you run over things quickly—you sweep them under the rug. "I'd be quite nervous about Monday because . . ."

CLIENT: Because I'd think, "Oh, I'm going to make mistakes"—that kind of thing.

ELLIS: And that would mean . . . ?

CLIENT: And that would mean that I was right all along—that I'm a jerk!

ELLIS: Now you see, you've just boxed yourself in completely!

CLIENT: Even if I get hired, even if it's a lousy job, they wouldn't have hired a jerk.

ELLIS: *Or*—"It's a good job, but I'm not going to be able to make it, and I'm a shit."

CLIENT: Yeah . . .

ELLIS: So you see, you've closed just about all of the exits in your head. If you get interviewed and aren't accepted you'll think you're a jerk, and that will prove what you've always believed since the age of nineteen: That you'd better not try to do things, because you're no good. And if you actually get the job, it'll either prove that the job . . .

CLIENT: They'll find out I'm no good.

ELLIS: That's right—they'll find out you're incompetent and no good, and that'll be a terrible thing. Now, unless you go over and over those two ideas . . .

CLIENT: The second one is that they'll find out I'm no good. What was the first?

ELLIS: The first one is related to their refusing you—that they'll find out you're no good while interviewing you.

CLIENT: Or else when I get hired they'll find out I'm no good.

ELLIS: That's right. Now, is there any exit with your views?

CLIENT: No!

In this portion of the transcript, Ellis shows the client how her self-rating issues will plague her whether she is rejected or hired with respect to a given job. This can be considered an example of his criterion for pervasiveness in psychotherapy, as he is helping the client to see the many manifestations of a particular form of irrational thinking to which she subscribes.

ELLIS: There'll be no exit from anxiety—that's the issue. Now, let's jump to the other thing for a moment—let's just suppose that you get a job, and you're doing okay at it.

CLIENT: Yeah—I always do very well on jobs, strangely enough.

ELLIS: Well—where do you get the jobs, if you do okay?

CLIENT: Well, somebody offers them to me. But I've never gone out and gotten one.

ELLIS: Right—but suppose you now have a job, and you're doing alright on it. It's not the greatest job in the world, but it's okay, and you're doing all right on it. Now, would you feel—after a while—the inertia, the not wanting to get up in the morning and go to work, and things like that?

CLIENT: Well, that happened to me two years ago! I worked for a year and a half.

ELLIS: Doing what?

CLIENT: Selling, in a boutique. And then I became the manager, sort of. And I did pretty well.

ELLIS: And why did you quit?

CLIENT: I just got bored with it. It was interesting to learn the business, but then it just got to be . . . there was nothing to do, and I had just gotten as far as I could go.

ELLIS: Yeah—so it really was a boring job . . .

CLIENT: Well, it was all right while I was learning it, but after a year and a half there wasn't much to do.

ELLIS: But you see, there were two avenues you could have taken there—one would've been to go look for another job—because the best time to look for a job is when you have one—and the second would have been to go open your own boutique or something.

CLIENT: That's what a friend of mine was trying to get me to do, and I got panic-stricken.

ELLIS: Because . . . ?

CLIENT: "Oh, couldn't do it, couldn't do it; it would fail, it would fail . . ." I got utterly panic-stricken.

ELLIS: Yeah, but where'd you get *that* nutty idea—"It would fail, it would fail"—when you knew exactly how to run a boutique. How would it fail?

CLIENT: Well—actually, I didn't have any knowledge of the business end of it, at all. I was just in charge of the sales girls and some of the stock—things like that. I didn't have anything to do with the business end of it.

ELLIS: But wait a minute—there's an obvious thing you could do. Do you know what that is?

CLIENT: Well . . . get a job someplace where I could learn the business end of it.

ELLIS: Right—why didn't you do the obvious?

CLIENT: Because I was a neurotic slob!

ELLIS: But that's vague, you see. Now you're going back to the vagueries.

CLIENT: Because I had no confidence that I'd be able to do it.

ELLIS: Well, you began as a saleswoman there, and then they let you run the place, and it got boring because it was easy for you. Now what's the evidence that you couldn't also learn to do buying, and pay bills, et cetera? What's the evidence for that?

CLIENT: None.

ELLIS: But you concluded that.

CLIENT: I concluded that—right.

ELLIS: And with every job you've ever had, somehow or other you did okay . . .

CLIENT: But I've always concluded that—I told you that before—that I was there under false pretenses, and they were going to find it out eventually.

ELLIS: But take that boutique job—what were the false pretenses? You were managing the thing and it became too boring, easy. So what were the false pretenses?

CLIENT: Well, I couldn't possibly learn to do the business end of it—I don't know anything about business.

ELLIS: (Unintelligible) . . . we're back now to the anxiety! You see, it doesn't look like real passivity and inertia in the sense that, "I just don't wanna work"—although there may be some of that in there, too.

CLIENT: Not so much—because I like *doing*, you know.

ELLIS: You like activity. But there's *extreme* anxiety . . .

CLIENT: I feel like I'm tearing in two directions! You know—wanting to do something and being terrified to do it.

ELLIS: The terror seems to be, one, "I'm going to be refused if I try for a job," two, "Even if I get it, I can't make it," and three, "Even if I make it, then it's a crummy job or there are aspects of it I never could do well at."

CLIENT: I'm just *determined* to be boxed in!

ELLIS: Well, you're determined not to explore the hypotheses that you are *able* to do more in life than you let yourself do, and that even when you fail at something, you're not a shit.

Here, Ellis again applies his criterion for pervasiveness by exploring the possibility that low frustration tolerance might be contributing to this client's job-related difficulties. This route, however, seems to lead back to the client's ego anxiety and self-rating issues. In relation to this, Ellis utilizes repetition in order to reinforce the message that failure is not evidence of one's worthlessness.

CLIENT: Well—how can I counteract it?

ELLIS: By asking, "How could I possibly be a shit?" There are four disputing questions that we give to everybody . . .[4]

CLIENT: Yeah—"What am I saying to sustain it; is it true?"

ELLIS: Right. "Where is the evidence, and what's the worst thing that could happen if I fail at this, whatever it is." If, for example, you went out and looked for a job and fell on your face—or if you got a job and failed at it—what's the worst thing that could happen? Now, you don't seem to be *doing* that about this area—asking yourself these questions and thinking them through to the right answer. You've indulged yourself all your life in the nutty conclusion that failure proves you're a shit.

CLIENT: So what you want me to work on . . . is that I can go ahead and fail, be turned down and fail, and I'm still not a shit!

ELLIS: That's right! Whether it's with regard to a job, or socially, or anything—you can't legitimately devalue *you* just because you've failed at something—and just because you may have failed many times.

CLIENT: Even though I *haven't* really failed at these things—you still think that's the thing I should work on?

ELLIS: Well, you haven't failed mainly because you haven't gotten yourself into anything complicated. In your whole life, what was the most complicated work you ever did?

CLIENT: Oh, I've had a lot of jobs . . .

ELLIS: What was the most *complicated*—where you really had responsibility and did a variety of things?

CLIENT: Um, never.

ELLIS: Well, you see—and yet on the . . .

CLIENT: Well, I ran a bar in Chicago.

ELLIS: Who owned the bar?

CLIENT: My husband and me—but I used to run it plenty of times when he was away.

ELLIS: So you did practically everything—buying, bartending, managing the employees, et cetera. Now, did you only do that because you were married?

CLIENT: Probably.

ELLIS: Because let's suppose you weren't married . . .

CLIENT: I never would have had the courage to go to Chicago and open a bar! (Laughs) You know that! I had somebody with me to do it—somebody to take care of me.

ELLIS: And did he have prior experience at that?

CLIENT: Oh, not much. But he was the kind who did all sorts of things like that.

ELLIS: So that time you had a fairly complicated job. You got into it through him, but then you made the wrong conclusions, again: "Unless some man is around and leading me by the hand, I can't make it at a thing like that."

CLIENT: I know it.

ELLIS: That's a nutty conclusion—because you could go right back to Chicago—assuming that you had the money—and do exactly the same thing without him. Why would you need him, now that you know that kind of business?

CLIENT: Well, I don't understand what I'm supposed to work on—am I supposed to work on the idea that I *won't* fail?

ELLIS: No . . .

CLIENT: I'm going to work on the idea that I can fail, and can get refused, and that I'm still not a shit.

ELLIS: That's right! But while you're working on that, you could also realize that somebody with your intelligence and experience could practically never fail completely. As I said before, if you tried enough interviews, you'd get a job. If you tried enough jobs, you'd succeed at some of them. But if you do fail, you're never a shit—you're never devalued as a human being. Now *that's* what you'd better work on, and I really mean work on it! Okay . . .

CLIENT: Thank you—see you Monday.

Ellis has provided the client with direct guidance in terms of teaching her how to dispute her irrational beliefs. He clarifies the nature of the irrational thinking that he would like to see her modify, and emphasizes the fact that she had better make independent attempts to work at overcoming it.

In concluding this chapter, it is noted that there are aspects of Ellis's criteria for efficiency in psychotherapy which could not be illustrated in the above transcript. Obviously, the application of his criteria for brevity, maintenance, and prevention could not be demonstrated, as the transcript represented a single session within an ongoing therapy process. Extensiveness in psychotherapy was also not illustrated, as the content of this session was focused largely upon the remediation of a particular emotional problem. If this client were to continue her therapy to the point of successful termination, it might be predicted that she would acquire the skills necessary to maintain (and augment) her therapeutic gains, prevent future emotional and behavioral problems, and enhance her potential to lead a more fulfilling life.

Finally, it is noted that Ellis made relatively little use of profanity during this therapy session. This observation can serve to illustrate the fact that he is capable of being quite flexible in his therapeutic work, as he will modify his approach to "fit" the profile of a given client. Profane language represents a tool for increasing therapeutic effectiveness, and in most cases Ellis is judicious in its use.

NOTES

1. This is the fairly well-known film in which Rogers, Perls, and Ellis are each seen providing therapy to a volunteer "client," Gloria. Ellis (1986b) has critiqued his own performance in this film. He believes that he was effective in terms of showing Gloria (in a "direct, no-nonsense manner") her perfectionistic and self-blaming philosophy. He also states, however, that he may have tried to present too much material in the brief time provided, and that he may have focused too much on her sentences and self-statements rather than on her meanings, evaluations, and images.

2. It is noted that while Ellis makes reference to most of these behaviors at various points in his writings, they have never before been listed in terms of a comprehensive review of his own use of force and energy in psychotherapy. The category of "Confrontation/Insistence" was devised by the authors as a means of describing a behavior that was frequently observed within his sessions.

3. According to Ellis and Bernard (1985), ego anxiety can be experienced when individuals maintain "absolutistic and perfectionistic demands that they personally perform well and be approved by others." Discomfort

anxiety is described as "arising from their absolutistic and perfectionistic demands that others do their bidding and that conditions be arranged so that they easily and quickly get what they demand" (p. 21).

4. The four disputing questions Ellis refers to here are included in the RET technique, Disputing Irrational Beliefs (DIBS). DIBS is described in the final chapter of *A New Guide to Rational Living* (Ellis & Harper, 1975).

9

The Use of Special Techniques in Psychotherapy

Unusually clever and unique methods . . . had better remain just that—unusual and unique. Run of the mill cognitive, emotive, and behavioral techniques that can be used with many clients much of the time will probably prove more economical and useful. (Ellis, 1985a, p. 159)

During most of his therapy sessions, Ellis's activities are focused mainly upon identification and disputation of irrational beliefs, direct teaching of alternative rational philosophies, and suggesting ways in which clients might put these new philosophies into practice in their everyday lives. In his view this focus is most likely to promote efficiency and effectiveness in psychotherapy (see Chapter 8), and has the greatest probability of producing genuinely beneficial outcomes for clients. He nevertheless espouses and practices a circumscribed form of technical (as opposed to theoretical) eclecticism,[1] and will occasionally incorporate within his work techniques more common to other therapeutic approaches. Thus, he will instruct clients in the use of his version of referenting exercises, operant conditioning techniques, progressive muscle relaxation, and self-hypnosis. These methods, however, are usually used only when they are seen to represent a means for supplementing the process of effecting therapeutic cognitive modifications.

Ellis's approach to eclecticism is described as circumscribed because there are a large number of techniques which he completely avoids using within his practice. Although some of these techniques may ultimately be useful in helping clients to attain certain beneficial insights, they are deemed by Ellis to be inefficient because of the substantial amounts of therapy time they usually require. Ellis views other techniques as largely ineffective, as in the final analysis he argues that they fail to assist clients in altering the dysfunctional belief systems allegedly responsible for their psychological problems. Finally, Ellis regards a number of techniques as being distinctly iatrogenic, in the sense that they have the potential to exacerbate the symptoms with which clients originally entered therapy. In the two sections that follow, Ellis's concerns regarding the inefficient, ineffective, and iatrogenic qualities of many currently-practiced therapeutic techniques will be reviewed. Further on, an illustration of the manner in which he incorporates one particular "special" technique—hypnosis—within RET will be presented.

INEFFICIENT AND INEFFECTIVE TECHNIQUES

Consideration of Ellis's writings on the use of techniques not common to RET indicates that he views particular methods as ineffective when they ultimately fail to help clients identify and alter their upset-producing irrational beliefs. Techniques are regarded as inefficient when they lack this particular criterion for effectiveness, and also when they require inordinate amounts of therapy time and client financial resources to produce desired results. Dream analysis, detailed explorations of clients' past histories, skills training approaches (without concomitant cognitive restructuring), and "distraction" methods (such as meditation and progressive muscle relaxation) can all be considered to fall into the category of therapeutic activities which Ellis largely views as being ineffective and inefficient.

With regard to dream analysis, it is noted that clients will occasionally wish to present dream material to Ellis. While Ellis typically does not appear to discourage them from doing so, he eschews the sort of detailed analyses pursued by Gestalt or psychoanalytically-oriented therapists. He will listen to the client's report concerning the dream, and will then attempt to relate it to some current issue or problem with which the client is dealing. The following excerpt, drawn from the beginning of the second session with a young male client, can be considered illustrative of this process:

ELLIS: What's doing?
CLIENT: Oh, I'm feeling pretty upset about some past issues.
ELLIS: Well, which past issues? Are you still feeling guilty?
CLIENT: Oh, yes—definitely. I don't really think you're into dream analysis, but I'd like to tell you about a nightmare I had the other night.
ELLIS: What happened in the nightmare?
(For the sake of brevity, the client's description of the dream has been edited.)

CLIENT: I dreamt that I had committed some awful crime, and that I was about to be executed.

ELLIS: That's a punitive theme. Do you think that you deserve punishment?

CLIENT: I guess on some level I do. I still have to work that out of my system, somehow.

ELLIS: The question is, what are you doing to give up your guilt? You see, guilt means that you're putting yourself down. You believe that you're a rotten person who deserves to suffer—that's what was happening to you in your nightmare. Whenever you're feeling guilty, it's because you're telling yourself that, one, "I did the wrong thing," and two, "Therefore, I'm a shit who should be punished!" Now, if you really worked on that and changed your philosophy, you'd stop feeling guilty!

Ellis has quickly shifted the focus of discussion away from the content of the dream to consideration of the guilt-producing philosophy which is manifested in its theme. The session proceeds with further focus upon this philosophy, and the desirability of subjecting it to active disputation.

Insofar as detailed exploration of the past is concerned, Ellis will provide explanations to clients concerning its relative merits and disadvantages:

CLIENT: Do you think it's worthwhile pursuing stuff in my background?

ELLIS: It's not really necessary. In my work with clients we often don't talk about their pasts at all—it can be too time-consuming. Also, even if there are aspects to your past experiences that could be considered significant, it isn't the past that's causing your present problems. That's where psychoanalysis is wrong! It's what you're telling yourself *about* those past experiences that produces your upsets. The analysts would merely focus upon the fact that you might have lusted after your mother, rather than on showing you that you're telling yourself, "I'm a louse for having lusted."

The advantage to exploring the past—when it's done to a moderate degree—is that sometimes it'll show you that you believe the same crap now that you did back then. So, you can sometimes increase your awareness of your present philosophy by seeing its history, and the points at which you probably invented it.

Here, it is apparent that Ellis doesn't place very great value upon the "psycho-archaeology" practiced by many psychoanalysts. In his view, it appears that exploration of the past is appropriate only when it might serve the function of highlighting the recurring patterns of emotional and behavioral dysfunction that would stem from the maintenance of well-entrenched irrational beliefs. Hence, it is not surprising that Ellis usually deals with *current* activating events and consequent upsets during his therapy sessions.

His inquiries into clients' backgrounds are quite limited in comparison with those conducted by therapists of many other schools, and generally yield just enough information to allow him to begin formulating (and testing) hypotheses concerning the severity of a given individual's disturbance and the specific nature of his or her shoulds and musts.

Therapeutic approaches that emphasize remediation of skills deficits—such as assertiveness training, instruction in conversational techniques, and various approaches to weight reduction and smoking cessation—are also regarded by Ellis as being ineffective and inefficient when unaccompanied by interventions aimed at cognitive modification. Clients in therapy frequently *do* present skills deficits in important areas, but also block themselves from implementing these skills by subscribing to irrational beliefs which produce anxiety, guilt, anger, and other self-defeating affective states. Hence, Ellis believes that effective therapy should address *both* the skills deficits and the emotional obstacles to successful implementation (Ellis, 1982, 1986c). He can thus be heard, for example, providing coaching in conversational skills to socially anxious individuals, while at the same time disputing their irrational beliefs regarding perfect performance and the possibility of rejection experiences.

Ellis's position regarding what he labels as "distraction" methods is essentially similar to his view on skills training approaches. As noted earlier, distraction methods (according to Ellis's classification) include various approaches to meditation and relaxation (Ellis, 1982, 1984b). They are seen as functioning to relieve clients *temporarily* from experiencing inappropriate negative emotions, as they represent a means to distract oneself from focusing upon one's irrational beliefs. They do not, however, serve as a vehicle for directly producing modifications in clients' self-defeating philosophies. Ellis hypothesizes that as a result, clients will be likely to create upsets for themselves once again when the particular distraction technique is not in use. In the following excerpt, Ellis provides a client with basic instruction in a relaxation technique, along with a caveat regarding its most appropriate use:

If you're having difficulty falling asleep because you're planning ahead for the next day, you can try to relax by thinking of something monotonous—that will usually help you get to sleep. I normally do it myself by concentrating on my own breathing, and by saying in consonance with each breath, "relax, relax, relax."

Now, if you're *worrying* about something you can do the same thing, because the relaxation will help to interrupt the anxiety. It won't get rid of it, though—it will only interrupt it temporarily. To really work on ridding yourself of anxiety, you can ask yourself, "What's the worst thing that could happen; why would that be awful," et cetera.

By emphasizing his belief that relaxation techniques only serve as a means to interrupt the experience of anxiety, Ellis maintains a focus on the importance of disputing irrational beliefs. Thus, he has provided the client with a procedure that can represent a useful adjunct to her therapy, but has taken steps to prevent her from becoming overreliant upon it.

IATROGENIC TECHNIQUES

Within the fields of psychotherapy and medicine, iatrogenic techniques are generally defined as procedures which either instigate or exacerbate a condition that interferes with the healthy functioning of an individual. Iatrogenic problems, then, are a direct (though unintended) result of efforts at treatment. In reviewing Ellis's writings on alternative approaches and techniques within psychotherapy, it appears that he views iatrogenesis as largely being the outcome of procedures which tend to validate and reinforce clients' irrational beliefs (Ellis, 1982; Ellis & Yeager, 1989). Thus, iatrogenic techniques will contribute to an individual's becoming more irrational, and hence more prone to experiencing significant disturbances of behavior and emotion.

Space does not permit an exhaustive review of the many psychotherapeutic techniques and approaches which Ellis considers to have iatrogenic potential. The following list, however, illustrates his views concerning the manner in which several currently-practiced methods can reinforce clients' irrational philosophies:

1. *Approaches which emphasize providing warmth and love to clients*: While such approaches may tend to keep clients in therapy and can serve to boost their self-esteem, they can create dependency upon the therapist and reinforce the idea that it is essential to have the approval of significant others (Dryden & Ellis, 1985; Ellis, 1982).

2. *Catharsis and abreaction techniques*: Approaches which encourage clients to vent suppressed emotions such as anger may contribute to their becoming more, rather than less, angry. Such ventilation can cause them to "practice" and subscribe ever more strongly to their anger-creating beliefs (Ellis, 1977e, 1982).

3. *Gradual desensitization techniques*: While many variants of this approach have empirically-demonstrated utility in countering phobias and other neurotic symptoms, they can tend to strengthen clients' beliefs that it is awful to experience emotional pain and/or work hard at changing. Flooding or implosive methods may be more effective and efficient in producing change, but generally involve considerably more discomfort and effort (Ellis, 1982, 1983b, 1985a).

4. *Approaches which teach clients to believe in and depend upon a higher power*: Some transpersonal approaches to psychotherapy and certain organizations (such as Alcoholics Anonymous) encourage individuals to utilize the power of a being or a force greater than themselves to overcome personal problems. This can serve to reinforce the belief that they are unable to improve through their own efforts, and that they need to depend upon this higher power (Ellis, 1985c, 1985d; Ellis & Yeager, 1989).

In addition to the above techniques and approaches, Ellis appears to regard some forms of hypnotherapy as also having iatrogenic potential. It is noted, however, that he occasionally employs hypnotic procedures with some of his clients. The section that follows will attempt to explain this seeming disparity, and will provide a transcript of one of Ellis's hypnotherapy sessions.

COMBINING HYPNOSIS AND RET: THE USE OF A "SPECIAL" TECHNIQUE

Ellis (1985a) has written that hypnosis and the use of strong suggestion may "sometimes prove to be inelegant techniques that may interfere with clients' independent thinking" (p. 59). This statement, however, does not represent his only grounds for criticizing this approach to implementing therapeutic change. The following excerpt, drawn from an audiotape of one of his Friday evening workshops ("Problems of Daily Living"), is his response to a member of the audience who asks for his position regarding the use of hypnotherapy:

> Clients will from time to time ask me to hypnotize them, but I talk most of them out of it. Hypnosis is mainly a cop-out, and the clients who ask for it are often looking for a magical solution to their problems. There is no magic—the most effective way for people to change is through hard work and practice!

This quote summarizes Ellis's view on the possible iatrogenic qualities of hypnosis. Like the gradual desensitization techniques, it has the potential to reinforce the self-defeating beliefs that pain and discomfort are terrible (and must be avoided at all costs), and that difficult problems can be resolved through relatively effortless means.

Given his stated position on the use of hypnotherapy, it might seem ironic that Ellis is a board-certified hypnotherapist who will occasionally employ hypnotic methods with a number of his clients. An examination of the manner in which he utilizes hypnosis, however, can serve to explain this apparent contradiction.

First, as implied in the above quote, Ellis does not use hypnosis frequently or indiscriminately. He prefers that clients apply his dictum concerning "hard work and practice," as he believes that this represents the best route towards effecting meaningful and lasting modifications in their personal philosophies. If, however, he has obtained evidence during the course of therapy that a given client is unlikely to assume active responsibility for disputing his or her irrational beliefs, and if this same individual also harbors the expectation that hypnosis is the main means by which he or she will improve, then he will consider making hypnotherapy a component of his treatment approach. By doing so, he may manage to circumvent a potential source of resistance and can utilize the client's expectancy in the service of therapeutic change. As he has previously written, "Resistant clients who *believe* that hypnosis works may allow themselves to change with hypnotic methods when they would not allow themselves to do so without hypnosis" (Ellis, 1985a, p. 59).

Secondly, it is important to note that Ellis combines hypnotic techniques with what he regards as representing some of the most important (and therapeutic) elements of RET. As such, his hypnotic suggestions can be heard to consist largely of the following:

1. Statements which underscore the nature of the irrational beliefs to which the client appears to subscribe,
2. Disputations of these irrational beliefs,
3. Statements which emphasize the client's ability to dispute these irrational beliefs on his or her own,
4. Descriptions of an alternative rational philosophy, and
5. Directives concerning activities which are likely to move the client in the direction of desired changes and facilitate subscription to a more rational philosophy.

Finally, Ellis transforms the use of hypnosis into a homework assignment in its own right. Clients are encouraged to tape record their hypnotherapy sessions with Ellis, in order that they might be able to review them repeatedly between sessions. An element of independent effort is thus built into Ellis's approach to hypnotherapy, and clients who might have been recalcitrant about implementing other types of homework may eagerly listen to their hypnosis audiotapes. Each time they do so, they provide themselves with an additional opportunity to combat their irrational beliefs.

The following transcript provides an example of the typical manner in which Ellis conducts a hypnotherapy session. In this particular case, the intervention is aimed at helping a middle-aged male client to overcome his problematic drinking behavior. It is noted that Ellis utilizes a form of progressive muscle relaxation as a hypnotic induction, and then employs suggestions regarding eye-heaviness as a means for "deepening" the client's relaxed state. Following this induction, he provides direct RET suggestions encompassing the components described in the above list:

All right, now we're going to do the relaxation procedure that I described to you earlier. I want you to try to relax as much as possible. First focus on your toes—tense them up, and now relax them, relax them, relax them. Think about relaxing your toes. Now, relax the rest of your foot—let it be fully relaxed—nice and easy and free. Focus on relaxing your toes and your feet.

Now go to your calves—let them just sink into the chair. Fully, easily, nicely relax. And then your knees—relax them, relax them, relax them. You can feel warm, free, and relaxed. Now your thigh muscles—let them sink into a nice, relaxed state.

Next, allow your whole pelvic region to relax—easy, warm, free, flexible—relaxed. And now your buttocks—let those muscles sink nice and easily into your chair. Now, your stomach muscles—let them feel relaxed, warm, easy, and free. Next, your chest muscles—take a slow, deep breath in, and then slowly breathe out. Relax, relax.

(Ellis continues directing the client to focus upon relaxing particular muscle groups.)

Finally, focus on your eye muscles—let your eye muscles relax, relax, relax. Your eyes are now getting into a nice, warm, relaxed state. They're getting heavier and heavier as you relax, relax, relax. You *want* to be relaxed—you want your eyes to become heavy. You're letting them go; you want them to become heavier and heavier and heavier as you let yourself sink deeper and deeper into a relaxed state.

You're only listening to the sound of my voice, you're focusing on relaxing your body, and you're blotting out all distractions. You want your whole body to be easy, warm, free, and relaxed. Your body is nicely out of the way, you can focus intently, and you want to stay in this state so that you can focus on what I'm going to tell you to do. You're going to remember this after you leave this state—for the rest of the day, for the rest of the week—remembering exactly what these instructions are.

Now, you're focusing on what happens when you're about to drink—remember what happens when you're about to drink. Hereafter, whenever you get the urge to drink, you're going to stop and think. You're going to ask yourself, "Why am I going to have this drink, why am I doing this destructive thing?" And you're going to *see* why you're doing it. You're going to see the horseshit you tell yourself that causes you to do it. You're going to see that you're telling yourself, "I *need* this drink." And you're going to question and challenge that and ask yourself, "Where is the evidence that I must have this drink?" And you're going to answer, "There *is* no evidence that I need this drink. It's going to make me feel better *temporarily*, but it's going to screw me in the long-run." You're going to look at the truth—that the drink is destructive.

It's *only* giving you temporary alleviation of pain. You're going to see that practically every time you take a drink, you're doing it for the immediate gratification. And again, you're going to stop and think and use RET and say, "Why the fuck *must* I have this drink? It would be nice to get rid of my pain and anxiety with the drink, but why *must* I have what I want?"

You're also going to see that you're telling yourself things like, "I can't do anything else to enjoy myself—I can only enjoy myself with alcohol. I *need* it, I *must* have this immediate pleasure." And you're going to again dispute this by saying, "Where is the evidence that I can't find much more constructive ways of enjoying myself?" And you'll see that the answer is, "There is no evidence— I *can* find less destructive ways to enjoy myself. I can act in a non-destructive way, and not only get temporary pleasure, but future pleasure— future gain which I'll *really* enjoy."

Whenever you get the urge to drink you're going to *stop* and *think* and *look* for the horseshit you're telling yourself, and you're not going to accept it. You're going to challenge it, dispute it, rip it up a thousand times and push away the drink as you push away the horseshit. This is what you're going to do over and over—stop and think and use RET. You're going to use RET to show yourself that you *can* do it, you do not *need* that immediate pleasure, you do not *need* what you want. You don't *need* the immediate gratification *and* the future damage! You're going to fully realize the damage, the costs of drinking—and not just focus on getting rid of the immediate pain. This is what you're going to do, day after day. You're going to listen to this tape, and you're going to do the disputing—whenever you get the urge to drink.

Now you feel nice, warm, easy, and relaxed, and you're going to listen to this tape every day for the next two weeks. You're going to get more and more relaxed as you listen. You're going to do better and better at focusing on the instructions on the tape, and at *acting* on them. You're going to stop and think, stop the bullshit, push away the alcohol and replace it with clear thoughts.

You feel nice and warm and free, and in a couple of minutes I'm going to count to three and tell you to get up, go back to living, feeling fully awake and alert and alive. You're going to remember what I've said, and you're going to focus on relaxing your body and sharpening your mind. One . . . two . . . three . . .

At present, Ellis's manner of combining RET with hypnosis has yet to be subjected to the types of empirical tests which would serve to validate its effectiveness as a means for implementing therapeutic change. In a recent article, however, he states his observation that approximately eighty percent of his hypnotic clients attained good results through utilization of their hypnosis audiotapes (Ellis, 1985e). Interestingly, in this same article Ellis wonders whether comparable benefits would be accrued if clients omitted the relaxation component of their tapes and simply reviewed the section containing RET instruction. The fact that he submits this as a question for research would seem to underscore his skepticism regarding the use of "special techniques," and his strong preference for a no-nonsense approach to resolving emotional problems.

NOTE

1. Therapists described as technical eclectics subscribe to a particular theoretical perspective on psychological disturbance but are willing to utilize treatment techniques derived from other schools. They attempt to use their theoretical base to guide their choice of alternative techniques. Theoretical eclectics, on the other hand, will draw upon several different theories in their attempts to understand and treat their cases. Ellis is opposed to both theoretical eclecticism and unselective technical eclecticism, as he believes that these approaches can result in less effective (and possibly iatrogenic) therapy.

10

The Use of
Humor in Psychotherapy

If human disturbance largely consists of overseriousness; and if, as in rational-emotive therapy, therapists had better make a hardheaded attack on some of their clients' fatuous thinking, what better vehicle for doing some of this ideological uprooting than humor and fun? (Ellis, 1977c, p. 263)

Ellis (1985a) concurs with Viktor Frankl's view that it is healthy for human beings to take themselves seriously and give meaning to the events and circumstances of their lives. As stated in the quote above, however, he maintains that *overseriousness* is a major factor behind most forms of emotional disturbance. From his perspective, this overseriousness results when individuals apply various strongly held irrational beliefs to themselves, others, and the world around them. Through this process, they self-defeatingly escalate their basic wants, desires, and preferences into absolutistic musts, shoulds, and have to's. Then, when conditions are other than what they rigidly believe they *must* be, they fall prey to awfulizing, global person-rating, and "I-can't-stand-it-itis" (Dryden & Ellis, 1987).

The circumstances and thinking of a woman who has just been turned down for an important promotion on her job can be considered as a hypothetical case example. If this individual were merely to take this event seriously (which would be logical, as it is in direct conflict with her desires to advance her career), then she would most likely experience only the appropriate negative emotions of sorrow and concern. These feelings could actually be quite functional, as they might motivate her to make attempts at redressing the situation in the future (such as trying to realistically evaluate and improve her work performance). If, however, she subscribes to certain irrational beliefs

("One *must* be adequate and achieving in at least one important area in order to be a worthwhile person"; "The conditions of one's life *must* be comfortable and convenient"), then she is likely to imbue this event with exaggerated significance and engage in the types of catastrophizing and negative self-rating that are frequently involved in anxiety and depression.

Soon after he began practicing RET in 1955, Ellis (1987c) noted that "almost all the irrational beliefs that my clients fervently held, and with which they were royally befuddling or befogging themselves, had a clear-cut humorous, ironic, and undelightfully perverse quality" (p. 268). He found that by utilizing techniques involving humor, he was able to assist clients in the process of seeing the illogical and frequently contradictory nature of their irrational beliefs. He has noted that humor can represent a particularly powerful means for accomplishing this end, as it works through cognitive, emotive, and behavioral channels:

> Cognitively, it presents new ideas to the absolutistic, rigid client in an insightful, hard-hitting way. Emotively, it brings enjoyment and mirth, makes life seem more worthwhile, and dramatically intrudes on gloom and inertia. Behaviorally, it encourages radically different actions; it constitutes an anti-anxiety agent in its own right; it serves as a diverting relaxant. (Ellis, 1977c, p. 269)

In addition to showing clients just how silly their irrational beliefs truly are, Ellis (1977c, 1985a, 1987c) has stated that humor can function in a number of other therapeutically-relevant ways. In particular, he has noted that it can serve as a:

1. *Novel teaching device*: RET often involves much didactic teaching and repetition of important points. Humor can serve as an effective vehicle for conveying rational concepts, while at the same time relieving the monotony of repetition.

2. *Means to help clients view their problems more objectively*: Humor can help clients to face their foibles and failings without making themselves unduly (and from the RET perspective, unnecessarily) upset. With humor, they can become more objective observers of their self-defeating patterns of thinking, emoting, and behaving, and can circumvent any negative self-rating that might impede therapeutic progress.

3. *Cognitive distractor*: Introducing humor into therapy sessions can have the effect of temporarily interrupting clients' disturbance-producing thoughts. The improved affect resulting from this distraction can allow clients to better focus on the content of the session.

4. *Means to demonstrate the B-C connection*: Clients can be shown that the improved affect associated with humorous techniques can be traced to changes in their manner of thinking about themselves and their circumstances.

5. *Vehicle for rapport-building*: The use of humor can be facilitative with regard to the client-therapist relationship. It may help clients to view their therapist as a fellow human being to whom they can easily relate, rather than as a cold, uncaring professional.

While Ellis certainly employs humor in his individual and group therapy sessions, he probably makes greatest use of it during his Friday evening workshop, "Problems of Daily Living." At this workshop, Ellis demonstrates the principles and techniques of RET with volunteer "clients" who are willing to discuss an emotional problem in front of the workshop audience. His humorous sallies usually begin immediately after a volunteer has taken his or her place next to him on the dais, and often seem to serve as a means for distracting this individual from the dysfunctional thoughts that could produce stage-fright, or performance anxiety. Ellis's comedic remarks also help to maintain the audience's attention and interest in the demonstration, and represent a dramatic way of conveying important points to both the audience and the volunteer.

In terms of the nature of the humorous techniques he employs during therapy sessions and public demonstrations, Ellis (1977c) has written that his "therapeutic brand of humor consists of practically every kind of drollery ever invented—such as taking things to extreme, reducing ideas to absurdity, paradoxical intention, puns, witticisms, irony, whimsy, evocative language, slang, deliberate use of sprightly obscenity, and various other kinds of jocularity" (p. 264). By his own estimation, exaggerated language and escalating things to extremes are the devices he employs most often. In the sections that follow, Ellis's utilization of a number of these forms of humor will be described. The first three techniques—exaggeration, highlighting of ironies and contradictions, and jokes and slogans—were chosen for review because of the frequency with which they were employed by Ellis in the audiotaped sessions which form the basis for this book. Two other techniques involving humorous elements—shame-attacking exercises and rational humorous songs—will be covered because of their prominent place within the literature and practice of RET. Subsequent to description of these techniques, an extended audiotape excerpt will be presented in order to more specifically illustrate the manner in which Ellis utilizes humor in his psychotherapy.

EXAGGERATION

During psychotherapy sessions, clients will often verbalize statements that provide strong hints as to the thinking that underlies their current emotional and behavioral problems. Ellis is quite sensitive to such statements, and will humorously amplify them in order to (1) show the client the form that his or her irrational beliefs might be taking, and (2) demonstrate, in a relatively non-threatening manner, the fallacious nature of these cognitions. Such exaggeration is accomplished not only through the content of his responses, but also through certain non-verbal cues such as voice tone and gestures. Thus, the following exchange might occur between Ellis and a client:

CLIENT: When I think about giving that presentation in front of all of those people, I really get nervous!

ELLIS: (Ominously drops voice and speaks in tremulous tone; pounds on arm of chair for emphasis) . . . because I N-E-E-D their approval . . . I can't *survive* without their approval—oh, what a shit am I!

Exchanges like this are frequently followed by client laughter, suggesting that Ellis's statement had the desired impact. This ploy enables clients to become more objective observers of their own thinking processes, and helps them to appreciate the specious nature of certain strongly-held views and attitudes.

Ellis will also use exaggeration to deal with clients who insist that their dysfunctional emotions or behaviors are completely automatic and not preceded by any form of thinking. The following excerpt, drawn from a session with an overweight young woman, illustrates his typical response to such an assertion:

ELLIS: What do you tell yourself when you stop yourself from dieting and put the extra food in your mouth? You tell yourself some horseshit—I already know what it is, but let's see if you can figure it out!

CLIENT: I'm not aware of telling myself anything—it just happens!

ELLIS: That's right! The food jumps into your mouth and forces itself down your throat! It can't resist you!

CLIENT: (Laughing) I guess I tell myself that I really enjoy eating!
(The session continues with Ellis teaching the client the difference between preferences and needs, and how she makes herself "need" to overeat by believing that she *must* have the things she enjoys.)

Ellis also achieves dramatic effects during therapy sessions by employing exaggerated terminology. The title "love slob" might be bestowed upon a client who makes himself needy within romantic relationships, in order to comically highlight the consequences of believing that, "One *must* have the love and approval of certain significant others." The perfectionistic client may be reminded that all of us are "fallible fucked-up humans," while the self-downing individual may be shown that she's erroneously labelling herself as an "R.P." (Rotten Person). None of these terms are employed in a pejorative or condemning manner, and they may motivate certain clients to make more vigorous efforts at relinquishing their irrational beliefs.

HIGHLIGHTING IRONIES AND CONTRADICTIONS

With many clients, Ellis will point out the absurd manner in which their irrational beliefs cause them to act against their own best interests or needlessly exacerbate their negative feelings about unfortunate conditions:

> Thus, I kept showing one of my stubborn clients how ironic it was that she railed and ranted against cold weather, and thereby made herself suffer *more* when it was cold. I showed another of my resistant male clients that the more he angered himself about the inefficiencies created by some of the people with whom he was working, the less he was able to devote time and energy to correcting their inefficiencies. (Ellis, 1985a, p. 54)

In listening to audiotapes of Ellis's sessions one could easily form the impression that he has extraterrestrial connections, as he will often make references to "Martian observers." Far from representing a manifestation of paranoid thinking, these references appear to be a favored means for confronting clients with the fact that their irrational beliefs contradict certain aspects of reality. In this next extract, Ellis employs this device with a middle-aged executive who frequently angers himself about the unreasonable behavior of his intimates and business associates:

> The reason you get angry is because you're telling yourself, "They shouldn't behave in that way!" But let's face it—that's the way they easily tend to be!
> Suppose a Martian comes down from Mars and asks me, "How are you doing with those clients of yours?" I'd say, "Well, I'm doing o.k., but I've got this nutty guy who—despite the fact that he's quite bright—keeps telling me that his wife shouldn't be the way she indubitably is, and that his boss shouldn't be the way *he* indubitably is." The Martian might ask me, "Do all Earthians say that?" and I'd reply, "They all do—they're all crazy!" That Martian would die laughing!
> How can people *not* be the way they indubitably are—which is frequently unreasonable, screwed up, and nutty!

While the highlighting of ironies and contradictions can be accomplished in a humorous manner, it is noted that Ellis most often delivers this intervention in a direct and straightforward way. Even when attempts at humor are apparent on his part (as when he employs the "Martian observers" device), clients do not always respond in a mirthful fashion. Client laughter, however, is not necessarily the best gauge of the utility of a given humorous device. Rather, the usefulness of such strategies is best judged on the basis of whether or not they accomplish their intended purpose. In the present instance, this purpose is to have clients become more aware of the manner in which they create emotional obstacles to reaching their goals. With such awareness, they are in a better position to work at removing these obstacles.

JOKES AND SLOGANS

Although hardly an inveterate joke-teller during therapy sessions, Ellis will occasionally recount humorous stories in order to illustrate the fatuous nature of irrational thinking or to educate clients concerning significant aspects of human behavior. With regard to the former purpose, Ellis has used the following anecdote to emphasize the absurdity of refusing to accept reality:

> I often tell this joke about Gracie Allen, from the days when she was on the radio. She's in New York, and she's talking on the phone to her Aunt Sophie in California. First she says, "Oh, Aunt Sophie—how are you? Oh, that's fine; you're doing very well!" Then she says, "And how's Uncle Louis? Oh . . . still dead!"

The next excerpt, drawn from a videotaped demonstration of rational-emotive group therapy, provides an example of an anecdote used to convey information about behavior in intimate relationships. One of the group members has reported that he makes himself feel guilty about the fact that he thinks of other women during sex with his wife. When he appears to resist the notion that such imagery is "normal," Ellis responds with the following joke:

> A couple had a good sex and marital relationship. They'd been married for 25 years, their children were grown-up and married themselves, and everything was fine.
> They decided, "Hell, it's our 25th wedding anniversary—we'd better do something special!"
> So they went for a gourmet meal, which they loved. They went to a Broadway show, which was great. They went dancing, and had a ball. When they finally got home, they started to make love.
> But neither one got very aroused or excited.
> Finally, after about ten minutes, the wife patted her husband on the shoulder and said, "Well dear, I guess on this night of all nights, you're having trouble thinking of someone else, too!"

With this story, Ellis emphasizes the fact that it is usually difficult to always maintain a high degree of sexual attraction to one's partner within a long-term intimate relationship. In addition, he manages to remove some of the stigma attached to imagining oneself with other partners during sex with one's spouse. Importantly, Ellis does not allow an opportunity for the content of his anecdote to be misinterpreted, as he uses questions to check group members' understanding of the points he wishes to make.

As noted in Chapter 6 of the first part of this book, Ellis employs therapeutically-relevant slogans in his work with clients. These catch phrases frequently have a humorous impact, and represent an efficient and novel means for conveying information about the principles and techniques of RET. It is probable that they leave a lasting impression on many clients, as evidenced by one of the author's (J.Y.) experience as a co-leader of Ellis's therapy groups. Within these groups, clients are encouraged to offer each other assistance in overcoming emotional and behavioral problems. Not infrequently, it was observed that part of such assistance would consist of a group member spontaneously repeating one of Ellis's slogans to a peer in order to communicate some relevant aspect of RET.

SHAME-ATTACKING EXERCISES

Shame-attacking exercises (or shame-attacks) were described in the introductory chapter of this volume as voluntary exercises in which clients publicly engage in behaviors normally considered as silly or foolish. By undertaking such exercises, clients can help themselves to overcome the anxiety and negative self-rating they may experience in association with acting poorly in front of others. Ellis employs shame-attacks in both his individual and group therapy sessions, and will gleefully suggest "a few of my more famous ones" to clients who have difficulty in designing their own:

> Go to a department store at a busy time and unashamedly announce the time at the top of your lungs: "It's 4:45 p.m. and all's well!"
> Go into a drugstore at a crowded hour and say to the clerk in a loud enough voice for everyone to hear, "I want a gross of condoms. And because I use so many of them, I think I should get a special discount!"
> Ride the subway and announce the stops in a loud, clear voice: "Forty-second street!" Then, stay on the train!

As can be seen from this brief sampling, Ellis's shame-attacks often have a distinctly humorous quality. This quality can make the prospect of acting foolishly less horrifying to many clients, as it helps them to appreciate the comic side of inept behavior. As such, clients who undertake shame-attacks may become less likely to denigrate themselves when they do perform poorly in the future.

The humor inherent in shame-attacks is particularly evident within the context of rational-emotive group therapy. When clients report their shame-attacking experiences to the other group members, they frequently elicit appreciative laughter and other forms of positive attention. Such responses can serve to convince especially reticent or resistant clients to attempt such exercises themselves.

RATIONAL HUMOROUS SONGS

According to his version of events, Ellis (1987c) became the hit of the American Psychological Association's 1976 annual meeting when he sang a number of his rational humorous songs during presentation of his paper, *Fun as Psychotherapy* (Ellis, 1977c). He found that his humorous song lyrics (set to a variety of famous tunes) were better received than the more serious rational lyrics he had previously composed, and he subsequently began to use them more frequently with clients and during his public workshops and presentations.[1]

As with the other forms of humor he employs in psychotherapy, Ellis (1985a) has stressed the cognitive, emotive, and behavioral aspects of his songs:

> Cognitively, they usually satirize and attack a major iB (irrational belief). Emotively, they are musical and rhythmical, since they consist of humorous lyrics set to well-known popular songs, and they have a distinct evocative and dramatic impact. Behaviorally, they're designed to be sung again and again by disturbed individuals until they internalize their rational meaning and tend to automatically think and feel the way the song is oriented. (p. 54)

Rational humorous songs exist for a host of client problems, including approval anxiety, depression, hostility, low frustration tolerance, perfectionism, and refusals to accept reality. The following is an example of a song designed to attack the type of perfectionism that can result when clients believe that they *must* do well at their rational-emotive therapy:

Perfect Rationality
(To the tune of "Funiculi, Funicula"
by Luigi Denza)
Some think the world must have a right direction
And so do I! And so do I!
Some think that, with the slightest imperfection
They can't get by—and so do I!

> For I, I have to prove I'm superhuman,
> And better far than people are!
> To show I have miraculous acumen—
> And always rate among the Great!
> Perfect, perfect rationality
> Is, of course, the only thing for me!
> How can I ever think of being
> If I must live fallibly?
> Rationality must be a perfect thing for me!
>
> (Lyrics by Albert Ellis, copyrighted 1977
> by the Institute for Rational-Emotive Therapy)

In a number of his publications, Ellis (1984c, 1985a, 1987c) has made reference to successfully utilizing his rational humorous songs in the treatment of clients in individual psychotherapy. Review of his audiotaped sessions, however, suggests that they are not a frequently-employed component of his therapeutic work. Nevertheless, he maintains that when clients sing these songs to themselves or teach them to others, they represent a useful supplement to the other self-help techniques of RET.

USING HUMOR IN THE TREATMENT OF DEPRESSION: A SAMPLE SESSION

Now that a number of the means by which Ellis introduces humor into his therapy sessions have been detailed, a partial transcript of a session will be presented in order to demonstrate actual implementation. The client in this session is a young woman who has become depressed and suicidal following her husband's recent exit from their marriage. She has been left behind with a daughter, and is extremely pessimistic about her chances of ever attaining the things she wants most in life. The session begins with brief assessment of relevant history:

ELLIS: (Reading from the biographical form completed by the client) "I'm extremely depressed, I can't find any purpose in life, my husband left me, and I am miserable alone." When did he leave you?

CLIENT: About three weeks ago.

ELLIS: And why do you think he left you?

CLIENT: I don't know. We never fought, or anything.

ELLIS: Well, were you upset and depressed before he left you?

CLIENT: No, I was very happy.

ELLIS: So he didn't give any reason?

CLIENT: Well, we had bad communication, I guess. He just said that he didn't love me anymore, and that he didn't like being married.

ELLIS: Was the lack of communication on his side, or your side, or both?

CLIENT: I think it was on his side, because I tried to talk to him and he never said that anything was wrong. He never tried to work anything out—nothing.

ELLIS: Well, why were you very happy living with somebody who didn't communicate?

CLIENT: Well, we had a nice relationship, I guess. It could've been better—I guess we could've talked more.

ELLIS: Yeah, well, obviously . . .

CLIENT: I thought that it was all right . . . it was all that I wanted!

ELLIS: Well, if he didn't want it, what makes you think you couldn't find somebody else who would?

CLIENT: I just don't have any confidence . . . and I don't think that I will.

ELLIS: Yeah, but where do you get the impression that you won't?

CLIENT: I don't know—because I'm older, and I'm heavy, and . . . (Tearful) I just wanted my husband and I'm very unhappy being alone.

Ellis starts the session by immediately making reference to the problems the client has reported on a biographical form completed just prior to the session. Then, he begins to assess her perceptions regarding the reasons for the break-up of her marriage. In the process of doing so, he elicits material that suggests the client is depressed because of negative self-rating and hopelessness that stems from her belief that she will never be able to find another partner. The following exchange occurs several minutes later in the session. Here, Ellis focuses on her feelings of loneliness and hopelessness:

CLIENT: It's just that I'm very lonely . . .

ELLIS: You're alone, but loneliness means aloneness plus shithood. Now, why are you putting yourself down for being alone?

CLIENT: I don't know—I guess I'm afraid to face the world . . .

ELLIS: Because you're probably saying, (Drops voice) "I'll get rejected and I'll never be able to make it—won't that be *awful!*"

CLIENT: You're right, I'm feeling sorry for myself. I feel like I don't have any fighting spirit!

ELLIS: Because you're most likely saying, "I can't do better!" You obviously *could* do better than him. That's very obvious, isn't it?

CLIENT: I lived in the shadow of my husband—like he was everything! He was intelligent and good-looking—everything that anyone could ever want . . .

ELLIS: (Drops voice, speaks in tremulous tone) ". . . for a shit like me—he was going to perfume my shithood!"

CLIENT: (Laughs) Right!

ELLIS: Well, that won't work! You can see that it won't!

CLIENT: But I can't find anything to help me go on . . .

ELLIS: "I refuse to! Until you give me my piece of taffy—called my husband, or some equivalent—I refuse to do anything else!"

CLIENT: (Laughs)

ELLIS: That's what I hear you saying.

CLIENT: That's how I feel—that's true.

ELLIS: I know—and that won't get you anywhere! Will it?

CLIENT: No, it won't! I think that maybe this is just like a giant tantrum I'm throwing . . .

ELLIS: That's partly it. Practically all neurosis is just a high-class name for whining. It comes from thinking that it's *awful* not to get what you want. Now, why is that incorrect—to believe it's A-W-F-U-L to not have what you want?

CLIENT: Because you can't always get everything you want—maybe you'll get something else!

ELLIS: Right—that's one reason—and what does *awful* mean? It doesn't just mean sad . . .

CLIENT: It means different things to different people . . .

ELLIS: What does it practically *always* mean if you think about it?

CLIENT: It means hopeless.

ELLIS: That's another thing—it means hopeless—and doesn't it also mean *more than* sad?

CLIENT: Yeah . . .

ELLIS: Well, how could anything be *more than* sad?

CLIENT: I'm not sure . . .

ELLIS: (Drops voice, tremulous tone) "But I *feel* it can!"

CLIENT: (Laughs) I feel like I just want to die . . .

ELLIS: I know—because you're saying, "It's *more* than sad; it's horrible, awful, terrible, and hopeless, meaning I can't *ever* get what I want!"

CLIENT: That's . . . I really feel that I'd like to die!

ELLIS: And if you believe that you can't *ever* get what you want; that it's hopeless, what's going to happen?

CLIENT: Well, you *will* die . . .

ELLIS: No, you won't die . . .

CLIENT: (Laughs) Well, I'd kill myself!

ELLIS: Yes, you could kill yourself, but then you most likely *won't* get what you want! If you thought that it was hopeless to get through school, you probably never would've done it!

CLIENT: I don't know how I got through school. To me, it's a miracle!

ELLIS: Yeah, and did you do graduate work?

CLIENT: Yes, I have a masters degree.

ELLIS: So how did you effect that miracle?

CLIENT: I don't know . . .

ELLIS: Well, *why* was it a miracle? Are you so stupid that you couldn't do it?

CLIENT: Maybe I'm *not* so stupid—but I . . .

ELLIS: I don't understand how you managed to get a masters degree if you're so stupid!

CLIENT: Well, maybe I'm not *that* stupid . . .

ELLIS: Ohhh . . . "but I'm not as bright as I *should* be!" Now, why *should* you be brighter than you are?

CLIENT: Well, I don't care about brightness. I really don't care about things like that . . .

ELLIS: ". . . as long as somebody *loves* me!"

CLIENT: (Laughs) Right!

ELLIS: "But where will I ever get anybody to love a shit like me!"

CLIENT: That's right!

ELLIS: Now, why are you a shit? That's a proposition—go prove it!

In this passage, Ellis begins reflecting some of the client's irrational thinking in exaggerated form. When he shows her how she was using her husband to "perfume her shithood" (i.e., confirm her worth as a person), she responds with laughter. As he continues on this humorously confrontative course, her prior tearfulness dissipates, and her affect starts to become more positive. It is also noted that Ellis employs two of his more well-known slogans to make powerful, concise statements regarding the origins of loneliness and neurosis (i.e., ". . . loneliness means aloneness plus shit-hood"; "Practically all neurosis is just a high-class name for whining.")

Even when the client makes reference to suicidal wishes, Ellis does not deviate from his strategy of gentle confrontation. Instead, he shows her how these wishes stem from her thinking that her circumstances are hopeless. He focuses on her negative self-rating, and challenges her to find proof that she is worthless.

The session continues with Ellis disputing the client's belief that she will never be able to find another male partner, and with his teaching her about the illogical nature of global self-ratings. Finally, he offers her encouragement regarding her ability to cope with her husband's leaving, become more self-accepting, and effectively pursue her life goals. In this next segment, Ellis deals with the client's contention that her depression is upsetting the rest of her family:

CLIENT: I'm making everyone miserable . . .

ELLIS: They're making themselves that way—they're taking you seriously. You don't *make* anybody miserable!

CLIENT: I must be . . .

ELLIS: They're meshuganes who are making *themselves* miserable. They're *choosing* to be miserable. They could just feel sad and say, "Too bad our nutty daughter is this way." But instead they're saying, "Ohhh, look what that bastard husband did to her! She can't stand it! Isn't that *terrible!*"

CLIENT: That's right.

ELLIS: That's *their* nonsense.

CLIENT: So it's *all* nonsense. Everything is nonsense—nothing means anything!

ELLIS: No, now you're thinking like the fox and the grapes. The fox can't get the grapes, so instead of saying honestly, "Shit, I can't get the grapes, I want the grapes, I'll go look for grapes elsewhere," he says, "Who wants the grapes? It's *all* unimportant!" We call that "sour grapes."

CLIENT: (Laughs) Right—I know the story!

ELLIS: Yeah—so don't jump from believing that nothing is *all* important— which is true—to believing that nothing is important *at all*. That's horseshit. Lots of things are important. It would be nice, and quite important, if you got yourself together and achieved a good relationship.

CLIENT: That would be nice, but I'd like to throw in the towel!

ELLIS: Where will that get you? Where will it get your daughter?

CLIENT: I know—if you kill yourself people will feel bad for an hour, and then they'll go on living.

ELLIS: Right—you fixed *them*! The world will turn, and what will happen to your daughter?

CLIENT: I wish I didn't have a daughter.

ELLIS: You could give her away!

CLIENT: (Laughs) I wouldn't give her away! I just don't really want to face the situation . . .

ELLIS: But if you stopped your horseshit, a year or two from now you could be quite *happy* with your daughter and probably with another man! You're *able* to be happy.

CLIENT: I'd like to just have another man.

ELLIS: I'd be glad to give you one on a silver platter, but the platter is empty at the moment!

CLIENT: (Laughs) You know what I mean! I'd like to make believe this is all a bad dream, and just have someone else . . .

ELLIS: But you *can* do that—you just can't do it this second! It's certainly not impossible to get another man—especially if you stop using your creativity to *manufacture* your own misery! Just look at how creative you are!

Consistent with his teachings regarding self-responsibility for one's own emotional disturbance, Ellis shows the client that her parents are causing themselves to be unduly upset about her misfortunes. When she jumps to the erroneous conclusion that "it's *all* nonsense," he responds by comparing her to the Aesopian fox that was unable to reach the much-desired grapes. This analogy serves to evoke further laughter, and allows Ellis to underscore the point that while nothing is sacred, many things are important.

The client again makes reference to suicide, but this time expresses a recognition that such an action represents a very poor solution to her problems. Ellis reflects this recognition, and reminds the client that killing herself would result in additional hardships for her young daughter. He is again very encouraging with regard to her potential for helping herself to become happier than she now is, and humorously highlights the fact that finding another male partner will require some effort and time. Ellis focuses again on the goal of self-acceptance as the session draws to a close, and assigns relevant readings as a homework assignment.

Despite the fact that this client entered the session in an extremely depressed mood, Ellis was able to effectively confront her with the dysfunctional thoughts underlying her disturbance. This confrontation was partly accomplished in a humorous manner, by amplifying and reflecting some of the client's irrational beliefs. This strategy for confrontation may have allowed the client to become a more objective observer of her thinking processes, and certainly appeared to contribute to an improvement in affect as the session progressed. As such, it is likely that she was helped to become more receptive to alternative ways of viewing herself and her unfortunate Activating Events.

While this excerpt serves to illustrate the potential benefits of bringing humor into therapy sessions, it is noted that humorous techniques are best not employed in too casual a manner. The following section details a number of concerns regarding the use of such techniques.

SOME CAUTIONS REGARDING THE USE OF HUMOR

Although Ellis views humor as having great potential as a means for helping clients to recognize and correct their tendencies towards irrational thinking, his writings imply that it is best used in a discretionary manner. He notes, for instance, that while he uses humor to attack his clients' irrational beliefs, he is careful not to use it to attack the clients themselves (Ellis, 1977c, 1987c). This is consistent with the rational-emotive position regarding the unconditional acceptance of persons: While it is possible (and appropriate) to rate beliefs, traits, and behaviors as good or bad, it is inappropriate and illogical to globally rate human beings on the basis of their characteristics. Rational-emotive therapists strive to apply this distinction in their work with clients, and attempt to convey it to them through both teaching and modeling. As such, therapists would want to make sure that clients do not misconstrue their humorous jibes as a personal lampooning, as this could communicate contradictory messages and reinforce the notion that it is possible to give global ratings to persons.

Ellis (1987c) has suggested that psychotic individuals—particularly those with paranoid schizophrenia—may be prone to misinterpret his rational humorous songs in an iatrogenic manner. This observation can probably be extended to include other forms of humor that might be used in psychotherapy, as well as other types of clients. Thus, some depressed individuals might tend to be hypersensitive to therapist remarks that could be construed as criticisms. Such remarks could trigger a sequence of self-downing cognitions that leave the individual feeling worse, rather than better, by session's end. Likewise, clients with severe anger problems might become hostile in response to comments regarded as sarcastic in nature. In any scenario, it is incumbent upon the therapist to monitor the impact of his or her attempts at humorous interventions. Misunderstandings can then be corrected, and the client's upsets can tactfully be used as an opportunity to reveal the presence and nature of irrational thinking.

A final caution concerning the use of humor in therapy sessions stems from Ellis's (1984d) paper concerning irrational beliefs that can block a therapist's effectiveness. When therapists bring a philosophy of self-indulgence to their therapeutic work, they may tend to overuse techniques which they find enjoyable, regardless of the effect these interventions are having on their clients. Humorous techniques may represent a particular temptation for the self-indulgent therapist, as they are fun to use and allow for an opportunity to display one's cleverness. Decisions regarding the use of any therapeutic strategies or techniques are, of course, most appropriately based on their potential benefit to the client, rather than to the practitioner.

NOTE

1. These songs are available in *A Garland of Rational Songs* (Ellis, 1977d), which is published as both a songbook and cassette tape. Consumer beware—Ellis is the singer on the tape!

11

Dealing with Resistance

Resistance, whether we like it or not, is one of the most important aspects of almost all psychotherapy. Even when clients are unusually cooperative and hard working, they still reach plateaus of improvement, fall back, and resist getting better or improving as effectively as they could. Whether their resistance is largely their own fault, or whether it stems mainly from therapists' deficiencies, the fact remains that it had better be handled and at least partly overcome. (Ellis, 1985a, pp. 194–195)

In fairly recent years, a significant number of behavioral and cognitive-behavioral theorists have turned attention to the problem of defining and overcoming client resistance in psychotherapy (Butler, 1983; Golden, 1983; Goldfried, 1982; Lazarus & Fay, 1982; Meichenbaum & Gilmore, 1982; Shelton & Levy, 1981). Ellis (1983c, 1983d, 1984e, 1985f) presented his own formulations (and practice propositions) regarding this phenomenon in a series of articles which first appeared in the *British Journal of Cognitive Psychotherapy*. These articles were later consolidated and published as his book, *Overcoming Resistance* (Ellis, 1985a).

In this book, Ellis writes that he is in overall agreement with Turkat and Meyer's (1982, p. 158) view that "Resistance is client behavior that the therapist labels antitherapeutic." He goes on to state, however, that this definition is too general to be of much clinical utility, and lists the various types of resistance (and their alleged causes) that he has encountered in his practice as a psychotherapist. Included in this list are a number of categories which Ellis (1985a, p. 10) refers to as usual or common sources of client non-compliance or resistance. These categories include resistance:

1. Created by fear of discomfort,
2. Related to fear of disclosure and shame,

3. Stemming from feelings of hopelessness,
4. Motivated by self-punishment,
5. Motivated by fear of change or fear of success (which Ellis reformulates as actually representing fear of subsequent failure),
6. Motivated by reactance and rebelliousness,
7. Motivated by receiving secondary gains, and
8. Stemming from clients' hidden agendas.

In Ellis's view, client resistance does not always reflect willful (though unconscious) attempts to thwart the therapist's ministrations. Most of the common sources of resistance noted above are conceptualized as being the result of particular irrational beliefs which the client holds. As per the rational-emotive perspective, these irrational beliefs contribute to inappropriate negative emotions and dysfunctional behaviors which can act as obstacles to therapeutic progress. These obstacles can be overcome through modification of the self-defeating philosophies which lie behind them. As an example, a client who subscribes to the irrational belief that, "I *must* have my therapist's acceptance and approval" may "create" resistance stemming from a fear of self-disclosure and shame. Such an individual is less likely to be honest and open about the problems he or she experiences, and will probably derive less benefit from therapy as a result. In order to circumvent this potential obstacle to progress, Ellis would probably employ various disputation strategies to show the client that the love and approval of significant others does not constitute a necessity.

In the following transcript, drawn from the third session with a young, unemployed male client, Ellis can be heard addressing several of the common forms of resistance which he details in his book on the subject. Here, they are seen to represent specific obstacles to the performance of tasks and the attainment of goals which are of importance to the client:

ELLIS: What's doing with you?
CLIENT: Well, something just came up today—I didn't want to come here because I felt I hadn't done enough on my homework.
ELLIS: And you were blaming yourself? It sounds like you were ashamed.
CLIENT: Yeah, that's it.
ELLIS: But let's assume that you didn't do as much as you could have on the homework—how does that make you a shit?
CLIENT: I guess I blamed my entire self, rather than just concentrating on the fact that I wasn't working on my resume.
ELLIS: Right. You might often procrastinate when it comes to doing certain important things, but we wouldn't even be justified in labelling you as a procrastina*tor*—because then we'd have to prove that you procrastinate on *everything* and would *always* do so. You may be a human being who often procrastinates—but you're never a shit!

Now, shame is really another name for shithood. When you feel ashamed, it's because you're putting your *self* down—not just your behavior. Procrastinating on your resume *is* a bad act, in the sense that it's self-defeating—but the irony is that you're defeating yourself even more by *blaming* your self for the procrastination! Self-blame is unlikely to help you stop procrastinating. On the contrary, it'll probably cause you to do it more. After all, it consumes time and energy. But that's the way human beings tend to be—they blame themselves when they've acted wrongly, and thereby abet the wrongness!

CLIENT: Right . . .

ELLIS: So we want you to accept *you* with the wrongness, and then to work on *it*!

CLIENT: Okay—that's a fine thing to say—but how do I do it?

ELLIS: Let me give you an example—we have a guy in one of my therapy groups who's trying to earn his Ph.D. degree. That's fine—but he's choosing to define himself as a worthless person until he gets the degree. Getting the degree will somehow perfume his shithood, and then he'll allow himself to think he's okay. Now, do you see how nutty that is? It's crazy to define your *self* in terms of any *thing*—good, bad, or indifferent. If you believe that, "I *must* get a Ph.D. degree in order to be a worthwhile person," what's to stop you from later believing, "I *must* be a Nobel prize winner?"

CLIENT: Well, people do set goals for themselves.

ELLIS: We're not objecting to this other client's goals—we're objecting to the fact that he ties the attainment of his goals to his feelings of self-worth. Again, once he gets the Ph.D., isn't it likely that he'll conjure up some other condition for self-worth?

CLIENT: I guess there's no limit—right?

ELLIS: That's right—there's no limit. And the reason there's no limit is because all *conditions* for self-worth are arbitrary. You could conceivably define yourself as good because you won the lottery, or because you were eight feet tall. You could pick anything! The tragedy is that most people don't see that *they* did the picking. If you're going to make a choice, you might as well choose to accept yourself unconditionally!

CLIENT: I guess I've always based my self-acceptance upon having other people accept me.

ELLIS: Yeah—you're saying you *need* their approval.

CLIENT: Right.

ELLIS: So you have two criteria there: One, "I must do things well," and two, "Other people must approve of me for doing them well." Right?

CLIENT: Well, I don't necessarily think that I must do things *well*—I just think that I must do them. My girlfriend thinks that I'm acting irresponsibly by not working harder on getting a job, and I tend to agree with her.

ELLIS: So according to both you and her, you're doing poorly. But it still sounds like you've got two elements in there: "I know I'm doing poorly and I'm no good," and, "She disapproves of me for doing poorly and I'm no good."

CLIENT: Everything adds up to my putting myself down.

ELLIS: Everything appears to add up to those two conditions—"I must do well, and I must be approved." You're demanding two conditions for self-acceptance.

Ellis begins this portion of the transcript by addressing the client's self-reported urge to avoid attending the therapy session. He quickly determines that this urge is connected to the client's perceptions regarding his deficient homework performance, which serve to trigger irrational beliefs resulting in shame and self-blame. Ellis regards feelings of shame as representing one of the usual sources of client resistance, and has written that clients often "find it uncomfortable to talk about themselves freely . . . and to confess thoughts, feelings, and actions that they view as 'shameful' . . ." (Ellis, 1985a, p. 12).

In the present instance, the client apparently pushed himself to be open and honest regarding his avoidance urges and poor performance on the prior session's homework. In order to prevent his identified feelings of shame and self-blame from becoming significant obstacles to therapeutic progress in the future, Ellis shows him that they are an outgrowth of his rigid, arbitrary conditions for self-acceptance. When these conditions are not met, negative self-evaluations are likely to occur. The neurotic solution to these negative self-evaluations is to avoid situations in which one might fail at some important task, and/or be subjected to criticism by significant others.

Ellis provides the client with direct teaching concerning the desirability of approaching a philosophy of self-acceptance, and models unconditional acceptance of persons by responding to the client's deficiencies in a non-condemnatory manner. With these interventions, he may make it easier for the client to attend his therapy sessions, pursue his job-search activities, and face the occasional disapproval of his girlfriend without becoming unduly upset. Once this issue has received some coverage and the client appears to understand that his "self-downing" is self-defeating, Ellis moves on to another topic:

ELLIS: Now, let's get back to the procrastination. What did you tell yourself to block your progress on the resume?

CLIENT: Well, a lot of different things.

ELLIS: What were the *main* things that stopped you from doing what you said you would do?

CLIENT: I think the main thing was that I would look outside and see how nice the weather was, and then I would go and do something outdoors. I went for the immediate pleasure.

ELLIS: So it sounds like your philosophy was as follows: "I *need* this immediate gratification, and it's *too hard* to buckle down and do what I said I'd do." Is that correct?

CLIENT: Yes—that's pretty much what I was telling myself. I think I'm just finding ways to sabotage my job-search.

ELLIS: Because again, "It would be too fucking hard to work at it?"

CLIENT: Maybe so.

ELLIS: You'll be better off if you really convince yourself that it's *harder* if you *don't* work at it. Your procrastination may give you immediate ease, but will it really give you any greater gain?

CLIENT: No, of course not—I need a job in order to get enough money to do the things I want. But there's another thing—I tell myself that even if I *do* send out resumes and go on interviews, I'll probably be rejected.

ELLIS: But now we're back to the ego-involvement and self-rating. If you were rejected, it sounds like you'd say, "I'm not doing well at getting a job— therefore I'm rejectable," and that you'd then put yourself down.

CLIENT: Right—it comes back to the same thing.

ELLIS: Well, we usually come back to these two basic things, which most people have: One, the self-downing which stems from believing, "I must do well, I must not be rejected," and two, the short-range hedonism—"It's too fucking hard; going out and looking for a job is too big a pain in the ass." We're not denying that it's hard, but it's not *too* hard— and you'd better really convince yourself that in the long run, it's harder if you don't go out and get yourself a job. You can push yourself to take the risk of facing the discomfort involved in job-hunting, to take the risk of getting rejected, while remembering that the final goal is to do better in life and enjoy yourself more—not to get a fucking golden rating!

In this segment of the session, Ellis focuses upon resistance stemming from fear of discomfort and fear of failure. The former type, as Ellis (1985a, p. 11) has pointed out, is related to "clients' short-sighted demands that they achieve the pleasure of the moment even though this may well defeat them in the long run." The latter type is a consequence of believing that it is an absolute necessity to succeed at important endeavors, as failure experiences provide evidence of one's lack of worth.

With regard to fear of discomfort, Ellis shows the client that by subscribing to the notion that the job-search is "too hard," he steers himself away from it and engages in activities which require minimum effort and offer immediate gratification. Ellis emphasizes that the resulting short-range hedonism is unlikely to produce desired outcomes, and the client acknowledges that employment is a requisite condition for pursuing some of the other things in life which are of value to him. The client's fear of failure is within the context of rejection at job interviews, and Ellis responds to it by again highlighting the role played by a philosophy of self-rating. As the client appears focused upon the self-defeating goals of having to prove (to himself and others) that he is a worthwhile person and of having to gain immediate ease, Ellis offers more rational, alternative goals: To work hard at doing better in life, in order to ultimately gain more satisfaction and pleasure.

It is perhaps important to note that in this particular session, Ellis enlists the client as collaborator in the process of overcoming sources of resistance. He accomplishes this by actively encouraging him to examine his thinking for irrational beliefs, as when he asks him, "What did you tell yourself to block your progress on your resume?" This approach can be viewed as having certain distinct advantages over more passive or indirect strategies for dealing with resistance, as it serves to define more explicitly the problems to be focused upon and facilitates the client's growth towards becoming a more effective (and independent) psychological problem-solver. When client and therapist work *together* in this fashion, the term "resistance" seems to lose much of the meaning that is usually associated with it.

Many clients, of course, cannot be so readily enlisted as collaborators in the process of removing obstacles to therapeutic progress. With particularly resistant individuals, Ellis may adopt a strongly confrontative stance concerning the consequences of refusing to face reality and work hard at therapy. As an example of this, he has described the approach he employed with a client who consistently refused to implement homework assignments designed to help him overcome his fear of riding in elevators:

> Knowing this man's great resistance to graduated homework, I said to myself, "Nothing will probably do any good as far as getting him to go through the anxiety of riding in elevators, but what have we got to lose? I think I'll be very strong and see what happens." So I said to him, very powerfully and with all the sincerity I could muster, "Well, seeing what your record of resistance has been so far, not only to RET but to the 15 years of therapy you had before I saw you, I would say that you only have two good possibilities to overcoming your self-indulged fear of elevators."
>
> "What are those two possibilities?" he anxiously asked. His voice was quavering and his hands were waving around in a clearly distraught manner.
>
> "One," I said, "get in those damned elevators at least 20 times a day every single day for the next 30 days. Yes! At least 20 times a day for the next 30 days! Or," I deliberately paused dramatically, knowing what my next highly significant sentence was going to be.
>
> "Or what?" he asked.
>
> "Or suffer enormously for the rest of your life! Yes, s-u-f-f-e-r—*suffer*! Forever! Which of these two will you choose?" (Ellis, 1985a, p. 109)

Ellis reported that as a result of this confrontation, the client finally pushed himself to undertake the implosive desensitization exercises which were suggested, and ultimately overcame his elevator phobia.

Ellis will modify his style to suit the clinical circumstances with which he is presented. Based on review of his audiotaped sessions, however, it appears that most of his interventions for dealing with resistance are cognitive in nature. In other words, they are heard to consist mainly of verbal disputations of irrational beliefs. Nevertheless, it is apparent that he also utilizes many elements of the emotive and behavioral techniques for overcoming resistance which he has detailed in his writings (Ellis, 1985a). Thus, emotive techniques such as unconditional acceptance of clients, strong language, and the utilization of dramatic anecdotes and stories are a frequent component of his therapy sessions, as are suggestions concerning behavioral homework assignments. In an overall sense, Ellis's activities during therapy sessions can be considered consistent with the practice propositions he offers in his publications.

12

How Clients View Their Therapy with Ellis

Often, my clients tell me that when they are trying to do something that they are afraid of, and are having great difficulty doing it, they literally hear my voice saying, forcibly repeating: "Now what are you afraid of? What the fuck difference does it really make if you get rejected? What's really going to happen to you that's so terrible?" and so on. And they then go and do the things they've been terribly frightened of doing. (Ellis, 1983e, p. 9)

While the psychotherapy literature abounds with case histories and descriptions of the therapeutic process related from the perspective of the practitioner, it is relatively rare to find published accounts of the *client's* view of psychotherapy. Unfortunately, this provides us with a rather incomplete picture of the manner in which psychotherapy works, and leaves us guessing as to the styles, strategies, and techniques which may impact most positively upon psychotherapy consumers.

The work of Albert Ellis is no exception to this state of affairs. It is true that he has described in great detail the manner in which he conducts psychotherapy, and it is also true that other psychotherapists have provided their responses to his approach through numerous critiques, debates, and reviews. To date, however, very little published material exists concerning the manner in which Ellis's clients experience their therapy sessions with him. This is a notable deficit, considering the fact that his style deviates considerably from that which is viewed as acceptable practice by a number of other therapeutic schools. The present chapter will attempt to address this deficit by providing selected responses culled from audiotaped interviews with twelve of his psychotherapy clients.

The interviewees were volunteers who responded to an invitation (posted in the lobby of the Institute for Rational-Emotive Therapy in New York City) to share their observations and reactions concerning their therapy experiences with Ellis. The authors of this volume considered this posted notice to represent the most appropriate means for soliciting interviewees, as it could not result in violations of confidentiality nor place undue pressure upon given individuals to volunteer. Volunteers were informed in advance of the purpose of the interviews, and provided their complete consent to have their responses published. They understood that all identifying information would be omitted or altered, and that they could choose not to answer any questions which they found to be intrusive or otherwise aversive. All interviews were conducted by the first author (J.Y.).

The sample of twelve interviewees was comprised of seven men and five women, with ages ranging from 29 to 61 years. As per the interviewees own reports, the following presenting problems were represented within this group:

1. Bipolar disorder
2. Depression
3. Relationship problems
4. Impulsivity
5. Child-rearing issues
6. Psychosomatic symptoms
7. Social anxiety and non-assertiveness

The period of time spent in therapy with Ellis varied considerably from individual to individual, and ranged from four months to seventeen years. It is noted that more recent clients tended to schedule appointments on a more frequent basis, while those who had "been in therapy" with Ellis for very long periods tended to see him only intermittently. They would, for example, schedule an appointment every few months or so. Six volunteers had had both individual and group therapy with Ellis, four had had only individual sessions, and two had only experienced his therapy within the group context.

It is, of course, likely that this group represented a biased sample, as all of its members maintained ongoing contact with Ellis's Institute in New York City during the period in which the interviews were conducted. All but two of the interviewees still considered themselves to be current clients of Ellis.[1] As such, it is improbable that the group contained any truly "dissatisfied customers." It is noted, however, that while a few of the interviewees had nothing but positive things to say about Ellis, most seemed to try to present a balanced picture of his therapy. In addition, one individual was consistently negative in his commentary upon Ellis's approach.

While the interviews were generally conducted in a conversational tone, the interviewer attempted to obtain responses to a number of specific questions which the authors considered to be of particular relevance.[2] As will be seen, these questions dealt with such issues as clients' initial reactions to Ellis's approach, the manner in which their perceptions of his approach might have changed over the course of their therapy, and the aspects of his approach which they found most and least beneficial. Taken as a whole, interviewees responses to most questions were noteworthy for their variability: What one individual viewed as being very helpful, another individual experienced as being somewhat aversive. It is probable that this variability was a function of such factors as clients' presenting problems, prior life experiences, and importantly, prior experiences with other forms of therapy. Here, then, are representative responses to the questions posed to the interviewees:

How Did You Come to See Ellis in Therapy?

"My first introduction to Ellis was at the Friday night workshop. I thought he was very interesting and very dynamic, even though I didn't know much about his approach. A year later I went back and volunteered to go up on the stage—he helped me so much in that brief contact, I couldn't believe it! I then joined a group, and from day one he helped me tremendously!"

"My boyfriend at the time treated me to a session with Ellis."

"An old friend of mine suggested that I see him. I was too depressed to make my first appointment, so I phoned the Institute to cancel. Ellis sent a message back that we could have the session over the phone—that really blew me away! The effect of that first session was to bring me back to myself, to help me escape from panic—I was tremendously impressed!"

"I originally heard him at [a local college], giving one of his razzle-dazzle talks. I thought, 'Jesus Christ, this guy is the best!' I then started coming to the workshops on Friday, and finally scheduled an appointment."

"I have been in therapy since I was eighteen, and I've been through the gamut of therapists—and it was just talk, talk, talk. A friend of mine knew about Ellis, and he suggested that I go—so I came to the Institute, and Dr. Ellis really changed my life."

"I tried insight-oriented therapy twice, and it didn't help me. I read one of Dr. Ellis's books, and I decided I would see him."

"I saw an advertisement for one of those Friday night sessions where Dr. Ellis interviews people, so I came to one of those and I volunteered. I was very pleased with the whole concept right away, so I joined one of his groups."

"A friend of mine recommended that I read *A New Guide to Rational Living*, and I was quite impressed by it. I called the Institute on a lark, and was quite surprised to find out that Ellis was still in practice—I thought perhaps he was one of those ivory tower guys. So, I made an appointment to come down and see him."

Can You Describe Your Reaction to Your Initial Therapy Session with Ellis?

"He would say things that would make me think—no other therapist ever made me think before! And some of the things he said made so much sense."

"I knew what to expect, because I'd read a lot about him. What I saw was sort of what I expected—kind of a cantankerous old man."

"He was simply there to hear what I had to say . . . he's not alarmed, although he's interested, at a certain workable level. By being this way, I think he somewhat quiets the potential panic in the patient."

"My first session with Ellis was a shock to the system. When I left the session I recall thinking, 'Wow, this guy is off his nut! He's different than he is on the platform [at the Friday night workshops]. In person, he goes for the kill.' But fortunately, I had the whole session on tape. When I listened to the tape later on, I thought, 'Look at that—he didn't say what you heard him say!' He may have used the words that I remembered, but the whole tone of what he said was called for, considering what I had said. Without the tape, I probably would not have come back."

"I'm sure that I saw him as being kind of crude, and too forward and all that stuff—but I know that I definitely felt better than I had in any other kind of therapy."

"Too confrontative, too forcefully rational, and shocking."

"Before I went, the things I had heard about Dr. Ellis didn't seem very encouraging—that he was not empathetic, that he comes across as cold and sometimes brusque. The first time I saw him, indeed he seemed detached—not apathetic, though. Very professional, but detached."

"My first impression was that he was just telling me things to make me feel good. For example, Ellis reassures you that you're a worthwhile person regardless of your performance. My evaluation of that was, 'No, damn it, you're really no damn good—he's just telling you you're *not* no damn good to make you feel better!'"

"I thought he was good because he was logical and interactive. He immediately pointed out some of the errors in my thinking and I said, 'Hey, I'm on to something here!' Usually when I left a therapy session [with prior therapists], I had more questions and doubts than when I came in."

Did Your Response to Ellis's Approach
Change as Your Therapy Progressed?

"I had mixed feelings—sometimes I'd say to myself, 'He's so cold—if only he'd have a little more warmth, I'd enjoy going to him more.' In the beginning it didn't bother me too much, because he helped me so much—but sometimes his coldness, his total detachment—I would find that unpleasant."

"It seemed that we developed a better capacity for rapport. As the sessions passed, I sensed that he respected me and found me interesting."

"There were times when I would trudge along on 65th Street after a session kind of wishing that he were more loving—because he doesn't purvey that at all. There are times when I could use a hug—but that's not his business."

"No—I liked his no-nonsense approach and felt that I benefitted from it, right from the start of my therapy."

How Would You Describe Ellis's Manner as a Psychotherapist?

"He didn't pretend to be nice—he'd lay back in his reclining chair, he'd pick his nose sometimes, he'd eat during the group, he'd yell at clients occasionally—he wasn't frightened of hurting someone's feelings. And I noticed he didn't encourage dependency."

"Detached, uninvolved—I don't think he gets any countertransference. Aloof, objective, like a scientist—looking at things objectively, without emotion."

"He doesn't come across as being a warm, caring person. He's a very results-oriented, 'cut the bullshit' type of person—but that's fine—I like that."

"Shocking—it's the craziest manner I ever saw in my life! I'm sure it was the first time I'd ever walked into somebody's grand office and confronted their sock feet—but my impression is that he doesn't give a shit what I confront—I didn't come there to see him display mid- to late-twentieth-century manners."

"I'd say strong, confrontative—even offensive. But he's an astute listener. More often than not, he'll smile very broadly at the right time."

"Brash, crass, direct, forceful, unrelenting, and humorous—or sarcastic—but I think that's very good. He never takes things *so* seriously—because when someone takes you real seriously, you tend to get more and more upset."

"Sometimes three-quarters of what you've just said is a pile of crap—he pushes that aside and gets to the stuff that's not a pile of crap."

"Very plebeian, very down to earth."

"He doesn't just let you sit there and build upon an irrational belief. If you say, 'I think I'm a shit,' he'll say, 'Prove it!' He debated with me, and I liked that interaction—it was something that I didn't get with other therapists, and it gave me something to think about."

Did Ellis Demonstrate a Concern for the Problems You Wished to Work On? If So, How?

"I sensed his involvement through the tone of his voice, the eye-contact, the body language, and his alertness."

"I really think that beneath the cold veneer, there's a very warm, caring, loving person. There were particular people in the group for whom he seemed to have more feeling or empathy. He seemed to feel for the people who were really trying to change themselves."

"He showed an interest. He would become very discursive upon a topic, and I suspected that the discourse was tailored for me."

"He'd show it in different ways—at times he seemed to get really pissed, and he'd bang the arm of his chair as if to bang a particular message into my head. I'd say to myself, 'Look at this guy, how totally interested and caring he is that he's getting this upset.'"

"What makes me know that he cares is that his memory is superb. How he remembers certain things about me, I'll never know."

"He pays you the compliment—which I think is pretty fucking rare—of paying attention, keen attention. You can be all the warm in the world, but if you're not really interested, piss on it—it's not going to work!"

"I keep marvelling at the fact that he's probably heard everything—in fact, I sometimes wonder why he's not burnt out. But he really cares—one time, for example, I said, 'I'm so unfocused in what I'd like to do for the rest of my life.' He quickly zeroed in on that, and didn't let me stray from the issue. He was very active and involved and led me from one step to the next."

"There were times when I'd come in and talk for almost fifteen or twenty minutes straight, and he'd sit and listen with his eyes closed. Then I'd test him—I'd say, 'Well, what do *you* think?'—and he would sit up straight and pick up right where I'd left off."

"I don't recall him ever showing any degree of concern—but I would sort of expect that from a therapist who sees hundreds and hundreds of people."

What Were the Aspects of Your Therapy with Ellis that You Found to be Most Helpful?

"He doesn't foster and encourage dependency. He purposely does not get friendly with clients—he's the only therapist I've ever known who works this way. I think that this makes people stronger, more independent. If he was very sweet and nice to me, I'd probably be running here all the time."

"He taught me that you have to work very hard to change your bad habits, and that it's not just something that's going to happen overnight. If you work very hard and are sincerely interested in making your life better, it can happen."

"His structure can be a positive—I like the fact that he allows each person in group just so much time to discuss a problem."

"He is there and he is open to any goddamn thing I may want to present. He's impossible to shock."

"The fact that he sticks to certain ideas. I might say to him, 'No, I can't do that,' and he'll say, 'Yes, you *can* do it,' over and over again. He makes sense, and he's given me tools with which I can help myself."

"I found it helpful that he really took an interest in my getting better— that he would apply all of his knowledge and experience to assist *me*! He seemed to have a commitment to helping me lead a better, happier life."

"There is nothing I feel reticent to talk with him about. I can say whatever I want, about whomever I want, and I trust him implicitly. I think that this is the most important part of my relationship with him."

"I've always thought his slogans helped me, because they can leap forward, they can hit me in the forehead: 'Oh yes, of course that's true!'"

"His philosophy of risk-taking—to do the things that you fear to do, and that nothing is as bad as you might imagine."

"Practicing being more logical—dropping all assumptions, and really looking at the situation in a logical way. I've come up with new, helpful philosophies since the time that I started seeing Ellis."

What Were the Aspects that You Found to be Least Helpful?

"I want to say the repetition of the rational sentences, but I know that that *does* help. Intellectually, I can see that if we've created crooked thinking by repeating it to ourselves all our lives, then the way to undo it is by repeating rational sentences—but sometimes in the group I would just get so tired of hearing, 'So, what are you telling yourself?'"

"Occasionally I wished his therapy were a little less cognitive, with a little more feeling involved."

"Interestingly enough, there are no negatives. He's even said to me, 'I can't be right all the time'—but so far, he's always been right on target with whatever he's told me."

"Sometimes in group I didn't think he was seeing us as individuals, with individual problems—more as just a mass of pretty much the same general problems that most of the population has—and for which the same responses would be given constantly."

"Maybe the fact that the time in the [half-hour] session is so limited. I have to choose my words carefully, and not go into too much detail. Sometimes I feel hampered by that, but at the same time I figure he's heard it all—so there's no reason to give him all the details."

"There will be times when I feel that I'm not resolving an issue and that I don't know quite where I am with it—so I leave the session in doubt. But is it not asking an awful lot to have *all* my toys repaired?"

"Sometimes I thought he was too distant and just making me into a number . . . and also when he's too forceful—I feel that's really unhelpful."

"I can't say that there was anything that would fall into the category of 'least useful,' because his therapy helped me immensely in my relationships, and helped me to become more independent."

"The least *likeable* aspect of his therapy could be his tendency to occasionally dismiss my concerns. He'll do a quick wrap-up at the end of a session which is, 'Well, you're doing just fine—keep up the good work.' Sometimes I don't think I *am* doing just fine, so when I hear that, I question it."

"It seems to me that Ellis does his very best work at his Friday night demonstrations. He's very aggressive about getting the person to respond and analyze their problem, and apply the RET principles to it. But he didn't seem to do that in his individual sessions with me."

What Would You Say Is the Most Important Insight You Acquired as a Result of Your Therapy Experience with Ellis?

"The thing that helped me the most is that I can accept myself now—I can't tell you how much that has helped! I think I can pretty much accept myself unconditionally most of the time—and just because I *choose* to! I still strive to do the best I can, but if I make a mistake, I make a mistake—I don't rate my self, my totality."

"I learned that nothing is truly awful—that you don't have to make anything all-consuming. He just kind of taught me to keep things in their proper perspective."

"The should and must issues have become a part of my conscious life. I've been helped by realizing that I have a right not to should all over myself."

"I try to look at myself and just accept myself with my imperfections and idiosyncrasies. I know that it sounds like I'm just parroting things that he's said, but they're so true! We don't have to end up with a rating of ourselves."

"The Oscar Wilde statement: 'Anything worth doing is worth doing badly.' That helped me to start taking on things, little by little."

"The world is as it is, and that I might as well accept it. I can still be happy in an unfair world!"

"That you can control your feelings by your attitudes—I'm not a slave to my feelings or to circumstances."

"I now have the capacity to recognize my value to myself."

"That it's your thinking that creates your feelings. Also, that there are no good or bad people—that people are not their actions."

"I became better able to accept myself—even when I was doing nothing to improve my circumstances. That gave me the ability to step out and do something. That was the main thing that helped me to really start changing."

Do You Recall Having Any Homework Assignments During Your Therapy with Ellis?

"He encouraged me to take risks . . . I was always very non-assertive, and he suggested that I become assertive—because if you wait for men or friends to come to you, you could wait a long time and have much less choice . . . I started going up to men that I found atractive, and it changed me from this passive, non-assertive woman into a person who goes after what she wants and has more choices."

"The one thing I really just *hated* was when he would ask all of the group members to do the yearly shame-attacking exercises. We'd have to tell him what we thought would be the most embarrassing situation for us, and then we'd have to go do those things. Mine was to yell out the stops in the subway—it was so stupid!"

"Well, he suggested that I try taking various courses of action, but he's never given me any homework assignments . . . he told me to read his books, which I did, feverishly."

"I never did much with the homework or the ABC forms. Maybe a couple of times—way back at the start of our association—he might have said, 'Try thinking this way or that.' But I really don't remember that very well."

"Only one time, when he suggested that I make an outline for a project I wanted to do. In fact, I wonder why he doesn't give me *more* homework. I thought I was supposed to get homework every week."

"There have never been any homework assignments between us, simply because I take so seriously the work that has to be done. At most he would say, 'Well, I think it would be a good idea if you did such and such . . .' So it was loose, because I'm a very responsible person."

"Sometimes he would say, 'Get a homework sheet from downstairs and fill it out.' When I did it, it helped me by the time I had completed it. But I felt the homework thing in group was kind of weak—I wish it had been more directed."

"He would give homework assignments at his Friday night demonstrations, but as far as I can remember he never gave *me* a homework assignment. I had the feeling he was burned out on homework assignments— maybe he thought it wasn't worth wasting his breath, because people wouldn't do them anyway."

"He's a big one on homework; it's part of how his method works. It seems to me that most of my homework assignments were centered around challenging my irrational beliefs—although I did have to *do* things, too. I remember I used to be fearful of making cold calls to customers at work— Al said, 'Just do it; pick up the phone and work through the fear.' He would often encourage me to do the things I was afraid of doing."

In What Ways Have You Changed as a Result of Your Therapy with Ellis?

"I've stopped blaming myself—and that was hard work. It doesn't come naturally to be rational."

"When I catch myself getting upset I say, 'Uh-oh, what are you telling yourself?' I check the validity of my beliefs, and I say to myself, 'Where is the evidence for this? Show me the proof!' This has helped me tremendously."

"I'm sober, and I'm dealing better with all aspects of my life. I see myself as being calmer in work and relationship situations . . . in fact, I've even been accused by some of my colleagues of being the quiet at the center of the storm—now *that* is amazing to me!"

"He's helped me with the job stuff . . . The fact that I've been working is a real change for me."

"I had been depressed for as long as I could remember. . . . By the third or fourth session, my depression was mostly gone. It's just amazing to me, how fast my depression lifted."

"I feel freer to be emotionally involved, because I now avoid a lot of self-downing. Previously, I had been a perfectionist."

"I think that I have a little more control over my life now—whereas before, I felt out of control. I've learned to look at things more intelligently and objectively, and I have less of a 'poor me' attitude."

"I used to criticize people a good deal—I'd think that people were wrong, and that they shouldn't be that way and so on . . . I'm much more tolerant in my attitudes towards people now."

"One of the key things I worked on with Dr. Ellis was overcoming the 'Icarus Complex.' Grandiosity had been my downfall. I learned not to 'risk the store,' and to be a little more cautious. I think I was a risk-junkie, and I learned to curb those tendencies."

"The shining jewel in the crown of my therapy was that I was able to get rid of my tension headaches. I used to get headaches as a punishment to myself, whenever I thought I'd done the wrong thing. But I learned that I don't have to give myself headaches—it's not the end of the world if I do something wrong!"

Which Was More Important for You in Terms of the Changes You Were Able to Make in Therapy: Ellis or RET?

"He's a kind of embodiment of his own theories. . . . One of the things I appreciate about Ellis is that he's an all-encompassing senior man. If some other therapist could bring that much dispassion to my news and show me how to put things in some kind of order and have a decent respect for myself—well, I could probably work successfully with that person."

"That's a difficult question to answer, because I've never worked with any other RET therapist. I think for me, it was probably a combination of both Ellis and RET."

"I think that RET is extremely helpful, but Ellis carries its weight."

"There's not another voice capable of repeating the concepts, the philosophy, the way he does . . . the man is the word. He *is* RET—to me."

"For me, they're almost synonymous . . . maybe RET more than the man himself—and I'm glad I'm saying that, because when he passes away, then what happens?"

"I think the two are intertwined. Just as Jerome Kern said that Irving Berlin *is* American music, I would say that Albert Ellis *is* RET. I don't think that I would have benefitted as much from therapy with some other RET practitioner, because Ellis is the originator of this system of thought."

"Far and away, RET is the answer to that question for me. The philosophy and concepts of RET are so on the mark, so valid, that they make all of the previous junk I had read on other therapies seem like pap!"

DISCUSSION AND CONCLUDING COMMENTS

In reviewing interviewees' responses to the first question above, it seems apparent that there are at least three main ways in which Ellis attracts potential clients. Some individuals attend one of his many public lectures or workshops, are impressed by his approach, and subsequently decide to schedule an appointment with him. Others have occasion to read one of his self-help books, are attracted to the therapeutic concepts contained therein, and decide to consult with the originator of those concepts. Still others have little or no prior exposure to his ideas or approach, but are referred to him by friends.

Interviewees described a variety of reactions to their first therapy contact with Ellis. Certain clients immediately took a liking to his "logical and interactive" style, while others experienced him as detached and "too forcefully rational." Whether or not they emerged from their first session with positive feelings for Ellis's style, however, all interviewees decided to schedule subsequent appointments with him. This may have been due to their expectancies regarding his utility as an emotional problem-solver; some clients, for example, reported that they had been helped significantly during their very first session.

Given Ellis's stated positions concerning the provision of warmth and love to clients (Dryden & Ellis, 1985; Ellis, 1982), it is not surprising that a number of interviewees experienced him as cold and detached during therapy sessions. These aspects of Ellis's demeanor did not, however, seem to be viewed as significant obstacles to therapeutic progress. Several interview respondents, in fact, speculated that additional warmth on Ellis's part could have had a deleterious effect upon their therapy, in the sense of creating and/or reinforcing feelings of dependency. Most clients appeared to believe that his "result-oriented," "no-nonsense" approach ultimately helped them to function more effectively as individuals.

The majority of interviewees felt that Ellis demonstrated a concern with helping them to overcome their emotional and behavioral problems, and they cited a variety of means by which he conveyed this concern. Some respondents made reference to his non-verbal behaviors during sessions (e.g., "the tone of his voice, the eye-contact, the body language"), while others emphasized his memory for details or level of attentiveness. Only one interviewee expressed the opinion that Ellis failed to demonstrate any degree of concern for his problems; it is noted, however, that this individual was consistently negative in his responses to the interviewer's questions.

With regard to the features of their therapy with Ellis that they found to be most helpful, many interviewees cited therapist behaviors and philosophic emphases which can be considered integral to the rational-emotive approach. This is interesting to note, as it seems to support the view that a therapist does not have to *be* Albert Ellis in order to practice effective RET. Interviewees made reference to a variety of features which they found to be least helpful; these included complaints concerning the relatively short length of individual therapy sessions (Ellis's are most often one-half hour long) and the frequent repetition of therapeutic messages. Perhaps as a result of this repetition and the brief time allotted for history-taking, two respondents felt that Ellis failed to treat them as individuals.

Almost half of the interviewed clients stated that the most significant insights they attained in Ellis's therapy were related to issues of global self-rating and self-acceptance. Clearly, they found his messages regarding the dysfunctional and illogical aspects of self-rating to be highly beneficial. This suggests that this message represents a critical component of Ellis's (and RET's) approach, and perhaps underscores the importance of explicitly addressing self-rating issues within psychotherapy. RET may have an advantage over other forms of cognitive-behavior therapy in this respect, as it places an emphasis upon the early identification and amelioration of such issues.

A number of interviewees were unable to describe any specific homework assignments given by Ellis during the course of their therapy. They recalled that he would occasionally suggest particular courses of action with regard to their problem areas, but they did not seem to view these suggestions as representing homework assignments. On the other hand, other interviewees were able to cite specific homework activities they had been assigned, such as shame-attacks and risk-taking exercises. While these disparities in clients' responses could suggest that Ellis is inconsistent in his utilization of therapeutic homeworks, it is also possible that particular interviewees maintained idiosyncratic definitions concerning the constitution of homework assignments. Some clients, for example, might mistakenly believe that rational-emotive homework consists solely of completing the Institute's self-help report forms (Sichel & Ellis, 1984). As such, any other suggestions concerning inter-session activities would not be identified as homework assignments.

In addition, as noted in Chapter 5, the content of the vast majority of Ellis's sessions is focused upon the teaching and demonstration of disputation skills. It is important to note that Ellis tends to deliver directives concerning the independent practice of such skills at various points during his sessions. As a result, clients who expect the assignment of homework activities to occur at a specific point in time (e.g., at session's end) may not recognize and label such directives as representing "genuine" homework assignments. This could, of course, contribute to client confusion regarding homework activities, and suggests that Ellis might obtain greater compliance with homework directives by explicitly labelling them as such.

All interviewees felt that they had experienced positive changes as a result of their therapy with Ellis. It is interesting that a number of them placed an emphasis upon *cognitive* changes, when one considers the fact that they probably did not enter therapy with "cognitive complaints." This observation would seem to highlight Ellis's skill at focusing his therapy upon the identification and modification of irrational belief systems.

Most interviewees had some difficulty in responding when asked whether they thought Ellis or RET was more important in terms of the changes they were able to make in therapy. As a few of them pointed out, they had never experienced RET with any therapist other than Ellis. Several, however, expressed the view that Ellis *is* RET. This is not too surprising, as Ellis is clearly identified as the founder of this therapeutic approach and is generally regarded as its foremost practitioner and proponent.

In concluding this chapter, it is again noted that psychotherapy consumers may have much to teach psychotherapy providers. Research dealing with the client's experience of psychotherapy could assist in identifying the most potent aspects of therapists' ministrations, and might lead to the development of more effective strategies and techniques. This is a fruitful area for much additional study, as it appears to offer substantial opportunities for refinements in practice.

NOTES

1. Two of the interviewees were currently seeing other therapists on the staff of the Institute for Rational-Emotive Therapy. One of these individuals seemed to express a preference for being involved with a therapist who displayed more warmth, while the other held the opinion that Ellis had not been forceful or direct enough in pointing out irrational beliefs.

2. While twelve individuals were interviewed, it will be noted that fewer than twelve responses are provided for each question. This is because interviewees occasionally failed to provide relevant responses to particular questions, or provided responses with very similar content. In order to promote readability and avoid redundancy, such responses were omitted.

13

Surviving as a Psychotherapist

I have seen myself at times doing the same thing over and over with clients and have recognized that this is a pain in the ass, this is something that I don't greatly like. But I have also looked at what I am doing in perspective, for I do like therapy as a whole, and I immensely enjoy those challenging cases that frequently come along. While I don't enjoy half so much the routine, nonchallenging cases, why do I have to enjoy every minute of doing therapy? I don't! (Ellis, 1972b, p. 119)

Albert Ellis has devoted his professional career to the practice, promulgation, and refinement of RET. He keeps an exceptionally busy schedule, and is almost always busy writing, reading, supervising trainees, or seeing clients. Given the fact that approximately 100 individual therapy clients and 50 group therapy clients will pass through his office in a typical week, it is likely that he logs more therapy hours than any other practicing psychotherapist.

How has Ellis managed to maintain this schedule (while remaining remarkably happy and generally quite healthy) during the course of a career that has spanned over four and a half decades? In an attempt to obtain the answer to this question and gain his views concerning other survival issues for psychotherapists, one of the authors (J.Y.) conducted the following interview with him:

YANKURA: Can you describe your typical psychotherapy schedule?
  ELLIS: My article, "My Philosophy of Work and Love,"[1] describes my usual daily schedule. It shows that I generally see clients from 9:30 in

the morning until 11:00 at night, with just a few half-hour breaks. That schedule includes my group therapy sessions—I lead five groups per week. On Wednesdays I conduct supervision with the Institute's psychotherapy trainees, and then on about fifty days each year I'm out of town giving talks and workshops.

Usually my individual therapy sessions are a half-hour long, and run back to back. As such, I would assume that I see more clients in a day than therapists whose sessions run forty-five minutes or longer.

Typically, I have a hundred individual therapy sessions in a week's time. About nine or ten of those are hour-long sessions; the rest are one-half hour long.

YANKURA: It sounds like you're considerably busier than most other therapists I know.

ELLIS: I would imagine that's true—certainly, most of them don't see clients until 11:00 at night. In addition, I have those five hour-and-a-half long group sessions that I mentioned a moment ago. In each of those groups I may see ten people—so you see, I see quite a number of people!

YANKURA: Have you maintained such a busy schedule throughout your career, or was it something that developed over the course of time?

ELLIS: Ever since I've been in full-time psychotherapy practice—beginning in 1952—my hours have started at 9:30 a.m. and have run until 11:00 p.m. So, this is a fairly old program of mine which I've maintained for over thirty-five years. Prior to 1952 I was employed as a psychologist by the state of New Jersey during the day; I had a part-time practice in New York City in the evening.

YANKURA: What are the means by which you manage to maintain such a busy schedule? Do you think that it's a result of your having an unusually high tolerance for frustration and discomfort?

ELLIS: I think that I was born with a very high energy level, and I tend to become bored when I'm not active.

As an example, I just recently underwent surgery for a hiatus hernia. I was in the hospital for nine days, and even after I was discharged I had to remain relatively inactive for a period of time. It was just about the most gruesome month of my life—I found it *boring* to lie in bed! Now I'm back to my regular schedule, and I can do the Friday night workshops, and I'm about to start my trips again.

So I would say that I was probably born with a very high energy level. Both my mother and father were very energetic people until their deaths—my father died at 80 and my mother at 93—and I *like* activity!

On Sundays I see no clients—but I'm busy most of the day! I'm either writing, or reading, or dictating letters. Again, when I'm not engaged in something like that, I tend to get bored. Of course, it doesn't *kill* me to be bored, but I don't like it.

I like activity, and I especially like problem-solving. During most of the time that I spend with my clients—both group and individual—I'm engaged in some form of problem-solving. I'm also relating to them somewhat, although I'm certainly not patting them on the head and having deep emotional relationships with them. I enjoy problem-solving, so my therapy schedule isn't as frustrating for me as it might at first appear.

At times my clients can get boring—that's one of the reasons I have half-hour sessions—and they can certainly be a pain in the ass by being late for their appointments, not doing their homework, et cetera. But I tend not to upset myself about such things because I have high frustration tolerance. My guess is that I have higher frustration tolerance than the vast majority of therapists.

YANKURA: Yes—that's my impression, too. Other therapists with whom I have contact frequently bemoan their busy schedules and the hassles of dealing with particularly difficult clients.

ELLIS: Well, that's another thing! When my really difficult clients—the borderlines and psychotics—fail to make progress, I don't get myself upset. I'd *prefer* these clients to work harder at their therapy and make more progress, but some don't—too bad!

I would guess that I'm less upsettable than many therapists with regard to the frustrations inherent in practicing psychotherapy. I'm able to accept myself, even if I *never* succeed with particular clients—I practically never put myself down. Although I think I'm okay at therapy, I can acknowledge that I'm not going to be as good with each client as some other therapist might be. That may be unfortunate, but I still don't have to put myself down.

Now, the fact that I'm often focused on refining the theory and practice of RET may also impact upon my ability to tolerate especially frustrating cases. Therapeutic failures tend to be very instructive for me—I can learn from my errors and failures, and modify my approach accordingly. This additional vector of my work makes it more interesting for me, and perhaps helps me to deal with the difficult cases somewhat more easily than therapists who aren't so concerned with developing a therapeutic approach.

YANKURA: Borderline and psychotic clients can be frustrating to work with because they may tend to make slow or minimal progress in therapy. Are there any other particular types of clients with whom you find it especially difficult to work?

ELLIS: In some ways, the most difficult clients are those who are disorganized or especially rigid in their thinking. They may be organic, psychotic, or near-psychotic. RET—and perhaps every other form of sound therapy—attempts to help individuals see how they're contributing to their own disturbance, and provides them with means for effecting helpful changes in their emotions and behavior. Disorganized thinkers have a difficult time with this. I have some elderly clients, for example, who don't concentrate well—sometimes they'll completely forget what we went over in previous sessions. So you see, these are among the most difficult clients.

Clients with anger problems can also be difficult to deal with. They may argue with you continually, and may do so in quite a hostile manner. Some of them actually seem to enjoy thwarting their therapists, which can make them less receptive to RET's rational-persuasive approach.

YANKURA: Other therapists with whom I have contact often speak of the difficulties involved in dealing with borderline clients. They report that they find these clients quite draining to work with, partly because of the hostility they may express towards the therapy and the therapist.

ELLIS: Well, I don't find them that draining for the reason I gave earlier—I don't *demand* of myself that I succeed with them. Some of them I may see for quite a length of time, and I can see that they're not utilizing the RET techniques or improving as much as I'd like. But I just assume that they're difficult because they're borderline, and I don't upset myself about their lack of progress. I don't demand that they not be difficult, and I don't demand that I should be helping them more. So, I don't really find them that draining.

YANKURA: Can you describe one particular case that you found especially difficult to deal with?

ELLIS: I can recall one particular male client whom I saw in group—the co-therapists and I had a difficult time getting him to approach and go out with women. We eventually *did* get him over that, to the point where he was at least starting to date. That was great progress! We also had a difficult time getting him to find a job, but he eventually did that, too. Then, he started complaining about the women he was dating—he said that they were only interested in money and in his having a better position than he had. He would do all right with them for a while, but he claimed that as soon as he let them know that he didn't make much money and had a low-level job, they would become critical and stop seeing him. We felt that there was probably more to the picture—that he had some manner that might be turning them off. While many women might prefer to date a man with more money and a better position, it's rather doubtful that all of them would terminate their relationships with him for that reason.

He rigidly refused to consider the possibility that he might be at least partly responsible for his dating difficulties, and became hostile with several of the group members who attempted to confront him on that issue. He just wouldn't accept what we were saying to him, and continued to blame the women he had dated in a very angry and perhaps paranoid fashion. We gave him homework assignments wherein we suggested that he monitor his behavior while out on dates, but he refused to do these assignments.

Since it seemed that we were getting absolutely nowhere with him,

I finally told him that he'd better not continue with the group. It seemed to be a waste of time for him, and some of the other group members were upsetting themselves over his negativism and rigidity and leaving the group because they found him so obnoxious. Incidentally, this client was trying to go with very high-level women— we were trying to get him to date women more similar to himself in terms of their economic status, but he refused.

So we said, "Come back to group after you've dated any woman five or six times and have made an effort to examine your own behavior." He returned to group a year later, *hadn't* dated any woman five or six times, and had completely forgotten that he'd been given that assignment!

He was one case that I can remember where he continually refused our homework assignments and fought verbally with other clients in the group. As he seemed to be deriving minimal benefits from his therapy, it appeared that he was just wasting his time.

YANKURA: Did that particular client ever provide you with opportunities to work on your *own* frustration or possible feelings of anger?

ELLIS: Yes, he did—he was at times very hostile to me as well as to some of the group members, and I certainly didn't like him. If he had been a friend of mine I would have cut him off—who needs that sort of thing? So, I would occasionally become overdetermined and get myself somewhat angry at him for pigheadedly holding his ground. But I worked on my demand that he should act in a less execrable manner, so that I rarely—I won't say never—angered myself about him.

One time, incidentally, he came to my Friday night workshop and kept going on about some point in an overdetermined manner. I told him to stick to the point, and just say what he had to say. He kept arguing with me, however, so at one point I did get myself angry at him and shut him up. But then I realized that I was angry, and not just displeased and determined—so I found him after the workshop as he was getting coffee. I made myself go up to him and admit that I was wrong in getting angry! I worked on myself to admit my own wrongness, and quickly got rid of my anger at him because I told myself that he *should* be the way he is! So in both the group and a few individual sessions, as well as that one Friday evening workshop, I worked on my own low frustration tolerance about him.

YANKURA: Clients *can* be frustrating in therapy—they certainly don't always do what we think it would be best for them to do. Over the course of the years, you must have been faced with many occasions when that was the case. Have you found that your tolerance for that sort of frustration has increased through the years, either through simple exposure or through your actively working to boost your frustration tolerance?

ELLIS: My tolerance for that type of frustration has increased through the years, probably due to a combination of the two things you just mentioned. As you said, I've been exposed to this a number of times—that in itself probably helped me to accept the fact that therapeutic work would continue to be difficult. But the other part—which I really have worked on at times—was showing myself that these people can often be a pain in the ass, but they *should* be a pain in the ass because they *are*, and I can tolerate them.

I may not like the way they behave, and I may show them aspects of their behavior that seem objectionable. I did that, in fact, with that fellow I referred to earlier at the Friday night workshop. While I was apologizing to him, I pointed out the fact that he had been overdetermined to make his point during the workshop.

So, I keep after my clients and I keep after myself. By keeping after myself and learning to accept the fact that some clients are just a pain in the ass—that's the way they are—I've raised my frustration tolerance over the years.

YANKURA: Have you ever come close to what might be referred to as "burning out," in terms of your work as a therapist?

ELLIS: There once was a period of several weeks when I was feeling rather unenthusiastic about doing therapy. That was the time during which I was taking Reglan, which is a medication sometimes prescribed for people with a hiatus hernia.

For the first time in my life, I really wasn't enjoying the work that much—I would look forward to the end of the day. As far as I could see, the Reglan slowed me down and made me feel somewhat close to burn-out! I think I was experiencing some adverse physiological reactions to the drug, which seemed to pass when I stopped taking it.

Now, it's possible that I may be making a connection that really didn't exist—I may have felt that way because I was telling myself some crap at the time. But it certainly seemed that that feeling of burn-out was correlated with the period during which I was taking Reglan.

YANKURA: And that was the one time that you experienced a loss of enthusiasm for your work as a therapist?

ELLIS: Right. Now, there have been a few other times in my life when I've simply taken on too many things, and I've gotten behind in my work. For a month or so, for example, I may have too many workshops, be very booked up with clients, and fall behind in some of the writing projects I've started. At those times I may feel what could be called a little burnt out, but my solution is to simply cut back on the number of activities in which I'm involved. I'll tell people that I won't be able to meet the deadlines for particular writing projects, I won't take on too much more, and I'll try to get back to my usual schedule. So occasionally I may get overloaded, and somewhat akin to or close to burn-out. I rarely find it serious, and I'm able to recognize that it's temporary—and I know that I'll take steps to modify it.

YANKURA: At those times, do you experience what might be referred to as the emotional concomitants of burn-out?

ELLIS: No—I get concerned and displeased about the fact that I'm over-loaded, but I don't get panicked or very anxious and I definitely don't get depressed. Again, the only time I can recall that I was close to depression was when I was taking the goddamned Reglan!

YANKURA: This next question is less personal: Are there any particular survival problems that rational-emotive therapists, as opposed to therapists of other orientations, are likely to encounter in their work?

ELLIS: Practicing RET can present certain disadvantages in terms of the therapist's financial survival. RET can help many clients to make significant progress in a relatively brief span of time. As a result, clients may be inclined to leave therapy after just a few sessions. They may, of course, be leaving prematurely in the sense that they could have benefitted more from their RET. Nevertheless, RETers may have to get more clients than other types of therapists who tend to keep their clients a longer time. Analysts, for example, may keep a client for ten years! So that's a hazard of RET—the more effective you are, or the more effective clients even wrongly *think* you are, the more you might have to push your ass to get more clients. Other-wise, you might have some difficulty making a living as a therapist.

Now, one of the potential *advantages* of being able to help clients in a few sessions is that they may refer their friends and relatives to you. I would guess that in RET, we get more referrals from former clients than do other forms of therapy. That might be some compensation for the possible disadvantage I just mentioned.

YANKURA: There may be another compensation as well. Hopefully, during the course of RET, clients are taught that the human predisposition towards disturbance is never *completely* ameliorated. Hence, they learn that it's okay to come back for additional therapy—they're not expected to be "cured." Frequently, in my experience, clients have returned for "booster" sessions.

ELLIS: Oh yes, that's right. I have clients that I only see a few times, and then a year or two later they return. Some of them say that they now recognize they'd better work harder at their therapy, because pre-viously they didn't put in that much effort. Right, they do come back for booster sessions.

YANKURA: Can you speculate on any particular types of survival problems that therapists of other orientations might encounter?

ELLIS: Well, there are some therapists who really—whether they acknowl-edge it or not—sort of give love to their clients. They act very warmly and supportively to clients almost all of the time, and I imagine that they may have particular problems with the difficult customers. The difficult customers don't appreciate the love the therapist is giving them, and may still act nastily and non-therapeuti-cally: They may continually come late for their sessions, refuse to pay their bills on time, et cetera. Very warm and loving therapists may be prone to get themselves quite frustrated with such clients.

Analytic therapists may see the same clients endlessly, year after year. Given the fact that they may see each client two or three times a week, you would think that they'd tend to get bored. I'd be amazed if some of them didn't!

Also, a naturally active-directive type of individual may have difficulty in practicing a form of therapy that requires him or her to be relatively passive. If *I* practiced a passive form of therapy—such as classical psychoanalysis—I wouldn't like it that much. That may, in fact, be one of the reasons that I designed RET to be an active-directive approach.

By the same token, a naturally passive individual—one who just prefers to listen and doesn't like to take chances and push clients—may have a hard time practicing RET or some other active-directive form of therapy. If therapists don't practice a type of therapy that conforms with their temperament, they may experience difficulty.

YANKURA: I was going to ask you if you thought there were any particular types of personality characteristics that might enhance an individual's survival as a psychotherapist, and we seem to be getting into that issue. Apparently, there isn't any one set of characteristics that a therapist must have; it's more a matter of finding the best fit between the therapist and the therapy.

ELLIS: Right—but there are at least one or two characteristics that almost all therapists could use. First, it's good if they have high frustration tolerance, because so many clients are resistant. They don't do their homework, don't pay their bills, and may generally be difficult to deal with. You're better off not being a therapist if you have low frustration tolerance!

Years ago I had a client who was a psychologist—he had his Ph.D. degree and did fairly well as a therapist. But he didn't like the repetition that's often involved in therapy—sometimes you have to go over the same material again and again because the client isn't changing that rapidly. Eventually, he gave up his psychotherapy practice for other activities within the field of psychology that he found more interesting.

Therapists had better have high frustration tolerance and be naturally suited to the helping professions. They'd better really be interested in helping people to solve their psychological problems. Also, they had best not identify themselves with how well they do with respect to helping their clients. If they do, they'll tend to make themselves disturbed.

Therapists had better also acknowledge the limitations of psychotherapy. It's *hard* for people to change; even non-resistant clients have a difficult time changing. Therapists had better not expect miracles, not expect quick changes, and be able to accept the fact that people will fall back. Even after clients get over their symptoms and get "cured," so to speak, they can easily fall back again. So, it's beneficial for therapists to possess the types of non-neurotic personality traits that will enable them to accept the difficulties of therapy.

YANKURA: What words of wisdom would you offer to novice therapists?

ELLIS: If they don't naturally have it, they'd better work to develop high frustration tolerance. I'd advise them not to be perfectionistic, in terms of demanding that they always do well with their clients.

I would also advise them to recognize the importance of "selling" themselves to clients. Sometimes, even therapists who are good at therapy don't seem to attract clients. In order to attract and keep clients, you have to engage in some degree of salesmanship—just being a good therapist is not enough.

I've seen several therapists who are quite good, quite well-trained, who just don't seem to get many clients. On the other hand, other individuals who are not that hot as therapists may get plenty of clients. So, therapists had better face the fact that psychotherapy often—not always—is a matter of knowing referral sources and doing things like giving workshops, writing, and publishing. You have to find ways of reaching the public if you want to attract clients, and some therapists don't like to work at that.

Young therapists will frequently say to me, "Well, now that I'm ready to start my practice, what do I do to get clients?" I'll tell them that one thing they can do is socialize—go to social gatherings, meet people, be friendly, and tell them that they're therapists. If they meet enough people socially, they'll find that after a while some of these acquaintances will refer friends and relatives who are having problems.

But some of these newer therapists will tell me, "I don't like to socialize and spend time that way! I'd much rather read or watch the ballgame," or something like that. And I'll say, "Well, that's okay—you're entitled to prefer those activities—but while you're reading or watching the ballgame you're not likely to get many clients!" So, young therapists had better consider the practicality of doing certain things—such as socializing, giving talks, writing, or getting on T.V.—in order to attract clients! You can be the best therapist in the world, but still have very few clients.

YANKURA: Are these activities that you engaged in heavily when you were first starting out?

ELLIS: At about the time that I was first starting out as a therapist, I wrote a number of professional papers. I made out a mailing list, and sent out reprints of these papers to friends and acquaintances from various parts of my life. This served to remind them that I was now a psychologist, and provided them with some idea as to the types of work in which I was engaged. I think that I got my first group of clients mainly through that activity. Then, I began writing for the public, giving talks to groups, getting on radio and T.V. whenever I could, and pushing myself in various ways. So I used a variety of things to bring in clients—and ultimately, clients led to other clients. Now, whenever I do a study of the source of my clients, I find that 70 percent or more are referred by other clients. At the beginning, of course, that wasn't the case—that takes a while to develop. Incidentally, psychologists whom I had never even met began to refer clients to me because they had read my papers. There are many things that can be done to help bring clients in.

YANKURA: Do you see your schedule changing at all in the near future? Do you see yourself becoming less busy, or perhaps more busy?

ELLIS: Well, I can't exactly become busier, because there's only a limited number of hours in a day—I'm not going to start earlier and end later! For years I've had this limit, if you want to call it that, of starting at 9:30 in the morning and ending at 11:00 at night. So, I'm not going to become *more* busy—I may become less busy because I might do other things. I could, for example, do more writing and see fewer clients.

I'm now seventy-four. If my energies lag as I grow older, I may end up deciding to start later and end earlier—that's quite possible. That won't mean, however, that I won't *want* to do as much as I'm now doing—it will simply mean that I may not have the energy to do as much. So, I may well cut down. At the age of *ninety-four*, I don't know whether or not I'll still be maintaining my current program!

NOTE

1. Ellis, A. (1983f). My philosophy of work and love. *Psychotherapy in Private Practice, 1*(1), 43–49.

Appendix: Suggestions for Additional Reading

While the authors believe that this book presents an accurate and thorough-going description of Ellis's approach to psychotherapy, they recognize that many readers may wish to pursue further study of this topic. In order to assist such readers, they have provided the following brief annotated bibliography. This bibliography suggests readings which: (1) describe Ellis's views regarding the practice of efficient and effective psychotherapy; (2) outline the manner in which the development of RET might have been related to Ellis's own personal development and experience as a psychotherapist; and (3) provide insights concerning Ellis's professional and personal life.

A number of the articles and chapters contained in this bibliography have been cited extensively within the text of the present volume. Reading them in their original form, however, may offer particular advantages to students of rational-emotive therapy. First, such readings will provide additional details and clarification concerning Ellis's views on sound psychotherapeutic practice. Second, reading Ellis's articles will provide exposure to his unique writing style—a dimension of his work as a psychotherapist which this book does not fully convey.

Ellis, A. (1979). The issue of force and energy in behavioral change. *Journal of Contemporary Psychotherapy*, *10*(2), 83–97. Ellis utilizes this article to emphasize the desirability of client "work and practice" in bringing about behavioral change within psychotherapy. He critiques transpersonal or mystical solutions to psychological problems, distinguishes between intellectual and emotional insight, and provides caveats regarding means for achieving emotional insight.

Ellis, A. (1980). The value of efficiency in psychotherapy. *Psychotherapy: Theory, Research, and Practice, 17*(4), 414–419. Ellis's views regarding the importance of efficiency in psychotherapy receive full treatment in this article. He discusses and defines what he considers to be the main criteria for efficient psychotherapy, which include: (1) brevity; (2) depth-centeredness; (3) pervasiveness; (4) extensiveness; (5) thoroughgoingness; (6) an emphasis upon maintaining therapeutic progress; and (7) an emphasis upon preventing the occurrence of future emotional problems. An illustrative case presentation is provided.

Ellis, A. (1982). Must most psychotherapists remain as incompetent as they now are? *Journal of Contemporary Psychotherapy, 13*(1), 17–28. In this paper, Ellis presents his views regarding a number of psychotherapeutic techniques and approaches which he regards as being iatrogenic and/or ineffective. He cautions against "unselective eclecticism," and presents criteria for the practice of effective and efficient therapy.

Ellis, A (1984). How to deal with your most difficult client—you. *Psychotherapy in Private Practice, 2*(1), 25–35. Ellis begins this article by first listing what he believes to be the personal characteristics of effective psychotherapists. He then discusses five irrational beliefs that he regards as typical obstacles to therapeutic efficacy, and offers techniques for overcoming these beliefs and becoming a more effective therapist.

Dryden, W., & Ellis, A. (1985). Dilemmas in giving warmth or love to clients (Interview). In W. Dryden (Ed.), *Therapists' dilemmas* (pp. 5–16). London: Harper & Row. Within an interview format, Ellis provides elaboration concerning his views on the potentially negative effects of providing too much warmth and love to clients.

Warren, R., McLellarn, R. W., & Ellis, A. (1987). Albert Ellis' personal responses to the survey of rational-emotive therapists. *Journal of Rational-Emotive Therapy, 5*(2), 92–107. This article reproduces Ellis's responses to a survey of rational-emotive therapists conducted by the first two authors. The text of the article is presented in an interview format, and allows Ellis to elaborate on some of his responses to the survey questionnaire.

Ellis, A. (1974). Experience and rationality: The making of a rational-emotive therapist. *Psychotherapy: Theory, Research, and Practice, 11*(3), 194–198. In this article, Ellis makes reference to a number of his own personality traits and developmental experiences as factors that impacted upon his formulation of some of the main technical and philosophical features of RET.

Ellis, A. (1987). On the origin and development of rational-emotive therapy. In W. Dryden (Ed.), *Key cases in psychotherapy* (pp. 148–175). London: Croom Helm. Ellis presents two key cases which assisted him in his formulation of the theory and practice of RET. The first case is cited as the impetus for his strong focus upon clients' "self-talk" in psychotherapy, while the second served to highlight the role played by low frustration tolerance in producing and maintaining emotional disturbance. Dialogue between Ellis and each of the clients in these two cases is reproduced for the sake of illustration.

Ellis, A. (1972). Psychotherapy without tears. In A. Burton (Ed.), *Twelve therapists: How they live and actualize themselves* (pp. 103–126). London: Jossey-Bass. In this lively chapter, Ellis describes some of his childhood experiences and presents a history of the manner in which he entered the mental health field. He discusses several ways in which he has utilized RET to good effect in his own life, and provides a specific example of the manner in which he used it to overcome feelings of panic, shame, and anger that he experienced following an episode of insulin shock.

Ellis, A. (1983). My philosophy of work and love. *Psychotherapy in Private Practice*, *1*(1), 43–49. Ellis uses this article to speculate about the factors that have contributed to his intense involvement in the practice and promulgation of RET for over 30 years. He reproduces what he describes as one of his "typical weekday working schedules," which serves to illustrate the manner in which he structures his professional and personal life.

References

American Psychiatric Association. (1987). *Diagnostic and statistical manual of mental disorders* (3rd ed., Rev.). Washington, DC: American Psychiatric Assocation.

Beck, A. T. (1976). *Cognitive therapy and the emotional disorders.* New York: International Universities Press.

Becker, I. M., & Rosenfeld, J. G. (1976). Rational-emotive therapy: A study of initial therapy sessions of Albert Ellis. *Journal of Clinical Psychology, 32,* 872–876.

Bernard, M. E. (1986). *Staying rational in an irrational world: Albert Ellis and rational-emotive therapy.* Carlton, Australia: McCulloch.

Bernard, M. E., & Joyce, M. R. (1984). *Rational-emotive therapy with children and adolescents: Theory, treatment strategies, preventative methods.* New York: Wiley.

Butler, J. F. (1983). Compliance enhancement procedures in clinical practice. *Behavioral Engineering, 8,* 49–57.

Danysh, J. (1974). *Stop without quitting.* San Francisco, CA: International Society of General Semantics.

DiGiuseppe, R. (1986). The implication of the philosophy of science for rational-emotive theory and therapy. *Psychotherapy, 23*(4), 634–639.

DiGiuseppe, R., & Miller, N. J. (1977). A review of outcome studies on rational-emotive therapy. In A. Ellis & R. Grieger (Eds.), *Handbook of rational-emotive therapy* (pp. 72–95). New York: Springer.

Dryden, W. (1986a). A case of theoretically consistent eclecticism: Humanizing a computer "addict." *International Journal of Eclectic Psychotherapy, 5,* 309–327.

Dryden, W. (1986b). Language and meaning in rational-emotive therapy. In W. Dryden & P. Trower (Eds.), *Rational-emotive therapy: Recent developments in theory and practice* (pp. 34–46). Bristol, UK: Institute for Rational-Emotive Therapy.

Dryden, W., & Backx, W. (1987). Problems in living: The Friday night workshop. In W. Dryden (Ed.), *Current issues in rational-emotive therapy* (pp. 154–170). New York: Croom Helm.

Dryden, W., & Ellis, A. (1985). Dilemmas in giving warmth or love to clients (Interview). In W. Dryden (Ed.), *Therapists' dilemmas* (pp. 5–16). London: Harper & Row.

Dryden, W., & Ellis, A. (1986). Rational-emotive therapy. In W. Dryden & W. L. Golden (Eds.), *Cognitive-behavioural approaches to psychotherapy* (pp. 129–168). London: Harper & Row.

Dryden, W., & Ellis, A. (1987). Rational-emotive therapy: An update. In W. Dryden, *Current issues in rational-emotive therapy* (pp. 1–45). New York: Croom Helm.

D'Zurilla, T. (1986). *Problem-solving therapy.* New York: Springer.

Ellis, A. (1957). Outcome of employing three techniques of psychotherapy. *Journal of Clinical Psychology, 13*(4), 344–350.

Ellis, A. (1962). *Reason and emotion in psychotherapy.* New York: Lyle Stuart.

Ellis, A. (1963). *Rational-emotive psychotherapy.* New York: Institute for Rational-Emotive Therapy.

Ellis, A. (1967). Goals of psychotherapy. In A. R. Mahrer (Ed.), *The goals of psychotherapy* (pp. 206–220). New York: Meredith.

Ellis, A. (1968). *Biographical information form.* New York: Institute for Rational-Emotive Therapy.

Ellis, A. (1971). *Growth through reason: Verbatim cases in rational-emotive therapy.* Palo Alto, CA: Science and Behavior Books.

Ellis, A. (1972a). Helping people to get better rather than merely feel better. *Rational Living, 7*(2), 2–9.

Ellis, A. (1972b). Psychotherapy without tears. In A. Burton (Ed.), *Twelve therapists: How they live and actualize themselves* (pp. 103–126). London: Jossey-Bass.

Ellis, A. (1973a). My philosophy of psychotherapy. *Journal of Contemporary Psychotherapy, 6*(1), 13–18. (Reprinted, New York: Institute for Rational-Emotive Therapy.)

Ellis, A. (1973b). *Humanistic psychotherapy: The rational-emotive approach.* New York: Julian Press. (Paperback ed., New York: McGraw-Hill.)

Ellis, A. (1976). The biological basis of human irrationality. *Journal of Individual Psychology, 32*, 145–168. (Reprinted, New York: Institute for Rational-Emotive Therapy.)

Ellis, A. (1977a). The basic clinical theory of rational-emotive therapy. In A. Ellis & R. Grieger (Eds.), *Handbook of rational-emotive therapy* (pp. 3–34). New York: Springer.

Ellis, A. (1977b). Rational-emotive therapy: Research data that supports the clinical and personality hypotheses of RET and other modes of cognitive therapy. *Counseling Psychologist, 7*(1), 2–42. (Also in A. Ellis & J. M. Whiteley [Eds.] [1979]. *Theoretical and empirical foundations of rational-emotive therapy* [pp. 101–103]. Monterey, CA: Brooks/Cole.)

Ellis, A. (1977c). Fun as psychotherapy. *Rational Living, 12*(1), 2–6.

Ellis, A. (1977d). A garland of rational songs (Songbook and cassette recording). New York: Institute for Rational-Emotive Therapy.

Ellis, A. (1979a). The biological basis of human irrationality: A reply to McBurnett and LaPointe. *Individual Psychology, 35*(1), 111–116.

Ellis, A. (1979b). The theory of rational-emotive therapy. In A. Ellis & J. M. Whiteley (Eds.), *Theoretical and empirical foundations of rational-emotive therapy* (pp. 33–60). Monterey, CA: Brooks/Cole.

Ellis, A. (1979c). The issue of force and energy in behavioral change. *Journal of Contemporary Psychotherapy, 10*(2), 83–97.

Ellis, A. (1980a). Rational-emotive therapy and cognitive-behavior therapy: Similarities and differences. *Cognitive Therapy and Research, 4*(4), 325–340.

Ellis, A. (1980b). The value of efficiency in psychotherapy. *Psychotherapy: Theory, Research, and Practice, 17*, 414–419.

Ellis, A. (1982). Must most psychotherapists remain as incompetent as they now are? *Journal of Contemporary Psychotherapy, 13*(1), 17–28.

Ellis, A. (1983a). Failures in rational-emotive therapy. In E. B. Foa & P. M. G. Emmelkamp (Eds.), *Failures in behavior therapy* (pp. 159–171). New York: Wiley.

Ellis, A. (1983b). The philosophic implications and dangers of some popular behavior therapy techniques. In M. Rosenbaum, C. M. Franks, & Y. Jaffe (Eds.), *Perspective on behavior therapy in the eighties* (pp. 138–151). New York: Springer.

Ellis, A. (1983c). Rational-emotive therapy (RET) approaches to overcoming resistance. 1: Common forms of resistance. *British Journal of Cognitive Psychotherapy, 1*(1), 28–38.

Ellis, A. (1983d). Rational-emotive therapy (RET) approaches to overcoming resistance. 2: How RET disputes clients' irrational resistance-creating beliefs. *British Journal of Cognitive Psychotherapy, 1*(2), 1–16.

Ellis, A. (1983e). With P. Krassner & R. A. Wilson. *An impolite interview with Albert Ellis* (rev. ed.). New York: Institute for Rational-Emotive Therapy.

Ellis, A. (1983f). My philosophy of work and love. *Psychotherapy in Private Practice, 1*(1), 43–49.

Ellis, A. (1984a). *How to maintain and enhance your rational-emotive therapy gains.* New York: Institute for Rational-Emotive Therapy.

Ellis, A. (1984b). The place of meditation in cognitive-behavior therapy and rational-emotive therapy. In D. H. Shapiro, Jr. & R. N. Walsh (Eds.), *Meditation: Classic and contemporary perspectives* (pp. 671–673). New York: Aldine.

Ellis, A. (1984c). Treating the abrasive client with rational-emotive therapy (RET). *The Psychotherapy Patient, 1*(1), 21–25.

Ellis, A. (1984d). How to deal with your most difficult client—you. *Psychotherapy in Private Practice, 2*(1), 25–35.

Ellis, A. (1984e). Rational-emotive therapy (RET) approaches to overcoming resistance. 3: Using emotive and behavioral techniques of overcoming resistance. *British Journal of Cognitive Psychotherapy, 2*(1), 11–26.

Ellis, A. (1985a). *Overcoming resistance: Rational-emotive therapy with difficult clients.* New York: Springer.

Ellis, A. (1985b). Expanding the ABC's of rational-emotive therapy. In M. J. Mahoney & A. Freeman (Eds.), *Cognition and psychotherapy* (pp. 313–323). New York: Plenum.

Ellis, A. (1985c). Two forms of humanistic psychology: Rational-emotive therapy vs. transpersonal psychology. *Free Inquiry, 15*(4), 14–21.

Ellis, A. (1985d). Why Alcoholics Anonymous is probably doing more harm than good by its insistence on a Higher Power (Review of *Alcoholics Anonymous*, 3rd ed.). *Employee Assistance Quarterly, 1*(1), 95–97.

Ellis, A. (1985e). Anxiety about anxiety: The use of hypnosis with rational-emotive therapy. In E. T. Dowd & J. M. Healy (Eds.), *Case studies in hypnotherapy* (pp. 3–11). New York: Guilford.

Ellis, A. (1985f). Approaches to overcoming resistance. 4: Handling special kinds of clients. *British Journal of Cognitive Psychotherapy, 3*(1), 26–42.

Ellis, A. (1986a). Do some religious beliefs help create emotional disturbance? *Psychotherapy in Private Practice, 4*(4), 101–106.

Ellis, A. (1986b). Comments on Gloria. *Psychotherapy, 23*, 647–648.

Ellis, A. (1986c). Thoughts on supervising counselors and therapists. *Association for Counselor Education and Supervision Newsletter*, Summer, 3–5.

Ellis, A. (1987a). The evolution of rational-emotive therapy (RET) and cognitive-behavior therapy (CBT). In J. K. Zeig (Ed.), *The evolution of psychotherapy* (pp. 107–133). New York: Brunner/Mazel.

Ellis, A. (1987b). The impossibility of achieving consistently good mental health. *American Psychologist*, 42, 364–375.

Ellis, A. (1987c). The use of rational humorous songs in psychotherapy. In W. F. Fry, Jr. & W. A. Salameh (Eds.). *Handbook of humor in psychotherapy: Advances in the clinical use of humor* (pp. 265–285). Sarasota, FL: Professional Resource Exchange, Inc.

Ellis, A. (1988). Psychotherapies that promote profound philosophical change foster behavioral change. *Journal of Integrative and Eclectic Psychotherapy*, 7(4), 397–402.

Ellis, A. (1989). Comments on Garfield's chapter. In M. E. Bernard & R. DiGiuseppe (Eds.), *Inside rational-emotive therapy: A critical appraisal of the theory and therapy of Albert Ellis* (pp. 221–223). San Diego, CA: Academic Press.

Ellis, A., & Becker, I. (1982). *A guide to personal happiness*. North Hollywood, CA: Wilshire.

Ellis, A., & Bernard, M. E. (1985). What is rational-emotive therapy (RET)? In A. Ellis & M. E. Bernard (Eds.), *Clinical applications of rational-emotive therapy* (pp. 1–30). New York: Plenum.

Ellis, A., & Dryden, W. (1987). *The practice of rational-emotive therapy*. New York: Springer.

Ellis, A., & Harper, R. A. (1975). *A new guide to rational living*. Englewood Cliffs, NJ: Prentice-Hall. (Paperback ed.: North Hollywood, CA: Wilshire Books.)

Ellis, A., & Knaus, W. (1977). *Overcoming procrastination*. New York: Institute for Rational-Emotive Therapy.

Ellis, A., McInerney, J. F., DiGiuseppe, R., & Yeager, R. J. (1988). *Rational-emotive therapy with alcoholics and substance abusers*. New York: Pergamon.

Ellis, A., Sichel, J. L., Yeager, R. J., DiMattia, D. J., & DiGiuseppe, R. (1989). *Rational-emotive couples therapy*. New York: Pergamon.

Ellis, A., & Yeager, R. J. (1989). *Why some therapies don't work*. New York: Prometheus.

Festinger, L. (1957). *A theory of cognitive dissonance*. Stanford, CA: Stanford University Press.

Golden, W. L. (1983). Resistance in cognitive-behaviour therapy. *British Journal of Cognitive Psychotherapy*, 1(2), 33–42.

Goldfried, M. R. (1982). Resistance and clinical behavior therapy. In P. L. Wachtel (Ed.), *Resistance: Psychodynamic and behavioral approaches* (pp. 94–114). New York: Plenum.

Grieger, R. M., & Boyd, I. (1980). *Rational-emotive therapy: A skills based approach*. New York: Van Nostrand-Reinhold.

Haaga, D. A. F., & Davison, G. C. (1989). Outcome studies of rational-emotive therapy. In M. E. Bernard & R. DiGiuseppe (Eds.), *Inside rational-emotive therapy: A critical appraisal of the theory and therapy of Albert Ellis* (pp. 155–197). San Diego, CA: Academic Press.

Hill, C. E., Thames, T. B., & Rardin, D. K. (1979). Comparison of Rogers, Perls, and Ellis on the Hill Counselor Verbal Response Category System. *Journal of Counseling Psychology*, 26(3), 198–203.

Hoellen, B., & Ellis, A. (1986). An interview with Albert Ellis. *Psychotherapy in Private Practice, 4*(2), 81–98.

Huber, C. H., and Baruth, L. G. (1989). *Rational-emotive family therapy: A systems perspective.* New York: Springer.

Kanfer, F. H., & Phillips, J. S. (1969). A survey of current behavior therapies and a proposal for classification. In C. M. Franks (Ed.), *Behavior therapy: Appraisal and status* (pp. 445–475). New York: McGraw-Hill.

Kelly, G. A. (1955). *The psychology of personal constructs* (Vol. 2). New York: Norton.

Lazarus, A. A. (1967). In support of technical eclecticism. *Psychological Reports, 21,* 415–416.

Lazarus, A. A. (1976). *Multimodal behavior therapy.* New York: Springer.

Lazarus, A. A. (1989). The practice of rational-emotive therapy. In M. E. Bernard & R. DiGiuseppe (Eds.), *Inside rational-emotive therapy: A critical appraisal of the theory and therapy of Albert Ellis* (pp. 95–112). San Diego, CA: Academic Press.

Lazarus, A. A., & Fay, A. (1982). Resistance or rationalization?: A cognitive-behavioral perspective. In P. L. Wachtel (Ed.), *Resistance: Psychodynamic and behavioral approaches* (pp. 115–132). New York: Plenum.

Levy, R. L., & Carter, R. D. (1976). Compliance with practitioner instigations. *Social Work, 21,* 188–193.

Maultsby, M. C., Jr. (1975). *Help yourself to happiness.* New York: Institute for Rational-Emotive Therapy.

Maultsby, M. C., Jr., & Ellis, A. (1974). *Technique for using rational-emotive imagery.* New York: Institute for Rational-Emotive Therapy.

McGovern, T. E., & Silverman, M. S. (1984). A review of outcome studies of rational-emotive therapy from 1977 to 1982. *Journal of Rational-Emotive Therapy, 2*(1), 7–18.

Meichenbaum, D., & Gilmore, J. B. (1982). Resistance: From a cognitive-behavioral perspective. In P. L. Wachtel (Ed.), *Resistance: Psychodynamic and behavioral approaches* (pp. 133–156). New York: Plenum.

Salter, A. (1949). *Conditioned reflex therapy.* New York: Farrar, Straus, & Giroux, Inc.

Saltzman, N., & Ellis, A. (1986). Clinical exchange. *International Journal of Eclectic Psychotherapy, 5*(3), 276–278.

Shelton, J. L., & Ackerman, J. M. (1974). *Homework in counseling and psychotherapy.* Springfield, IL: C C Thomas.

Shelton, J. L., & Levy, R. (1981). *Behavioral assignments and treatment compliance: A handbook of clinical strategies.* Champaign, IL: Research Press.

Shostrum, E. L. (Producer). (1966). *Three approaches to psychotherapy* [Film]. Santa Ana, CA: Psychological Films.

Sichel, J., & Ellis, A. (1984). *Self-help report form.* New York: Institute for Rational-Emotive Therapy.

Strong, S. R., & Matross, R. P. (1973). Change processes in counseling and psychotherapy. *Journal of Counseling Psychology, 20,* 25–37.

Turkat, D., & Meyer, V. (1982). The behavior-analytic approach. In P. L. Wachtel (Ed.), *Resistance: Psychodynamic and behavioral approaches* (pp. 157–184). New York: Plenum.

Walen, S. R., DiGiuseppe, R., & Wessler, R. L. (1980). *A practitioner's guide to rational-emotive therapy.* New York: Oxford University Press.

Warren, R., McLellarn, R. W., & Ellis, A. (1987). Albert Ellis' personal responses to the survey of rational-emotive therapists. *Journal of Rational-Emotive Therapy, 5*(2), 92–107.

Weinrach, S. G., & Ellis, A. (1980). Unconventional therapist: Albert Ellis. (Interview). *Personnel and Guidance Journal, 59*, 152–160.

Wessler, R. A., & Wessler, R. L. (1980). *The principles and practice of rational-emotive therapy.* San Francisco, CA: Jossey-Bass.

Wiener, D. N. (1988). *Albert Ellis: Passionate skeptic.* New York: Praeger.

Wolpe, J. (1959). *Psychotherapy by reciprocal inhibition.* Stanford, CA: Stanford University Press.

Index